Motorbooks International Illustrated Buyer's Guide Series

Illustrated HARLEY-DAVIDSON BUYER'S ★ GUIDE™

Second Edition

Allan Girdler

A tip of my black and orange helmet to *Cycle*, *Cycle World* and *Road Rider*, for letting me borrow their photos and root through their files, and to Armando Magri, Mike Shattuck, Robbie Robertson, Lee Mueller, Len and Brad Andres, Nancy Girdler and the elusive Fischer brothers, whose patience was without limit.

First published in 1992 by Motorbooks International Publishers & Wholesalers, PO Box 2, 729 Prospect Avenue, Osceola, WI 54020 USA

Library of Congress Cataloging-in-Publication Data
Girdler, Allan.
Illustrated Harley-Davidson buyer's guide / Allan Girdler.—2nd ed.
p. cm.—(Motorbooks International illustrated buyer's guide series)
Includes index.
ISBN 0-87938-634-7
1. Harley-Davidson motorcycle—Purchasing. I. Title. II. Title: Harley-Davidson buyer's guide. III. Series.
TL448.H3857 1992
629.227'5—dc20 92-16635

On the front cover: Two of the greats from The Motor Company, separated by forty-plus years of tradition. In the background, the 1941 Knucklehead owned by Bob Kwiatowski of Anaheim, California. In the foreground, the 1988 Low Rider Custom owned by Lee Mueller of Westminster, California. *Ron Hussey*

Printed and bound in the United States of America

Contents

Preface

One day in the summer of 1954 I got a call from the sort of friend my mother used to warn me about. He wanted me to help him look at a used motorcycle, presumably because two heads are better than one, although in this case our collective motorcycle knowledge could have been expressed mathematically as two times nothing.

But I'd always sort of liked the motorcycles I'd seen from afar, so off we went. We listened as the owner indicated the ignition switch, the choke and the kick-start lever.

My friend applied the choke, flipped the switch and jumped on the lever. He hadn't known to check if the transmission was in neutral, which it wasn't. The engine boomed, the bike leaped forward, down the driveway, into the owner's garage and up the back wall.

My pal had lost interest in motorcycles before they hit the ground. He'd thoughtfully put himself below the bike as it fell backwards, so he was bruised and the motorcycle was unscathed.

And I was fascinated. I insisted on a complete tour of the controls and a lecture on the theory behind them. I paid the asking price ($50) and wobbled away, somehow managing to get home upright.

The motorcycle was a Harley-Davidson VL, a flathead 74 with hand shift and foot clutch. It was twenty years old and I was seventeen.

That was a long time ago.

Since then I've ridden a Mustang delivery trike and Honda's astonishing (if unsuccessful) NR500 Grand Prix racer. I've been across the US and Europe. I've ridden, repaired, tested and owned hundreds of motorcycles for hundreds of thousands of miles. I've been astride the best from Japan, Spain, England, Germany and Italy.

Parked in my garage as I write this are three Harley-Davidsons.

I like Harleys.

That isn't to say I understand why, not exactly, not in so many words.

Part of it must come from the continuity: None of the parts comprising my present bikes will fit that first machine but the 1970, the 1986 and the 1987 are air-cooled V-twins, just as the 1934 was. And when you see or sit on or hear either one, the reaction is and has always been, Gosh! A motorcycle!

Harleys are different. Not always better or worse than the other makes, but different. And this is a matter of the heart. As in all such matters, if you like something, you don't need to understand why, and if you don't, you won't understand either.

So. When the publishers asked if I'd be interested in this project, a buyer's guide for Harley-Davidsons, I said I was the perfect man for the job.

Oh, they said, because you know everything?

No, I said, because I don't know everything. For thirty years I've read wonderful stories I can't confirm, heard casual references to models never described in print. When I was building my bike I was amazed to discover how many people claiming knowledge were actually bluffing. The facts left out of the magazines weren't there because the writers didn't know them.

Thus, I was the best man for the job not because I knew it all but because I wanted to know it all. I had the perfect alibi. I could go to runs and swap meets, hang around the dealerships, pore over the old books and magazines and say it was work.

While I honestly hope I've answered your questions here, I can say with even more honesty that it's been great fun answering mine.

PS: My show bike is an XR-750, a 1970 engine in a 1972 frame. Took me three years to collect and assemble the parts, install the street equipment and persuade the state motor vehicle department to issue a license. Not for sale, but I predict you'll have as much fun finding and working on your own.

Allan Girdler

Harleys as a Collector Bike

Harley-Davidson has a fascinating history. Folklore holds that poor ol' Harley has stumbled along since 1903, making V-twins and nothing else, always half a generation behind current practice.

Folklore is wrong. Not only did Harley-Davidson not invent the V-twin, the company was in business building singles for six years before borrowing, so to speak, the logical vee from somebody else. Harley has made two-strokes as well as four-strokes, boxer twins as well as vees and at least three experimental fours, one inline and two vee. Not only did Harley's four-valve racing engines precede the Japanese system, Harley was making four-valve heads before a Harley exporter taught the Japanese how a modern motorcycle factory works.

Incredible but true. Quite a saga, but this isn't the place for it. All those wonderful machines from the distant past are beyond the scope of this book. The belt-drive singles and boardtrack racers and legendary JD sport bikes and flathead twins with wicker sidecars are appreciated in both senses of the word. They are true collector items. Even if all the dusty barns hadn't already been searched, if you found one of those really antique machines, you'd pay a small fortune to own and restore it. Even then, you could only ride it on special and sheltered occasions.

That's not what owning motorcycles means to most of us. So the subject here will be Harleys that meet the definition of that lamentably useful word, affordable. We'll be looking at the new and used models available in stores and through your neighborhood shopper or the classified ads. With few exceptions (to be detailed at the proper time) they will be Harleys priced for the enthusiast budget; that is, only a bit more than we can afford but manage somehow to justify.

This is possible, not incidentally, because of a Harley-Davidson principle that is out of step with the times. It's based on an industrial philosophy established prior to the invention of the annual model change.

Once upon a time, manufacturers assumed that the folks who bought their products wished to keep them. The products were therefore designed to be rebuilt, for as long and as often as the owner pleased. Changes were made only for improvement. Models were kept in production as long as they were in demand. When changes were made, they were made to allow retrofitting—installing the better parts on earlier models.

This principle, allied with customer loyalty unmatched in the world, means that the ordinary owner can get the parts needed to keep the old Harleys on the road. If the factory doesn't supply it, an accessory firm does. If the exact replacement isn't out there, the same part from a different year or model will fit. If it doesn't, it can be made to fit.

So by intention the 1992 FLT with V2 engine descended from the 61E of 1936. The V2-powered FXRS came step by step from the 1971 FX and the 1992 XL-1200 Sportster is based on the K model of 1952.

Thus, the first part of the story begins not with the first Harley-Davidson of 1903 but with the 61E; other parts will begin with the K, the racing KR, the 125 two-stroke of 1948 and so on. We'll see how they began, how they changed, what the weak and strong points were, how they can be upgraded and what to look for when you're in the market for one.

About the above nomenclature: The factory has always used letters to designate the various engine and model lines. Some of this is easily explained. The first overhead valve V-twin was called the E, and the 74 cu. in. version of that engine became the F. Naturally, because the same basic engine still appears in the current versions of that big twin, those models began with F, as in FLT or FXR. In the same way, that first Sportster engine was assigned the letter X, so all current Sportster models begin with X. Likewise, when the factory used the F engine and

The author, whose pride obviously has overcome his modesty, at Harley-Davidson's Ride-In Show, Daytona Beach, 1985.

frame with Sportster front end and styling, the model was designated the FX. Logical, eh?

Except that some of this logic has been clouded by time. Sometimes R means racing, as in KR or XR, and sometimes it means rubber mount, as in FXR. The letter C has been used for both competition and classic.

The letters have become an unwritten language, in that you can learn it by rote but you can't understand it through analysis.

Never mind. The letters stood for something, so because the line of descent is still generally in effect, this book is organized on the basis of the letters.

We will consider big twins, from 61E to FLT; Super Glides, from FX to FXRT; Sportsters, from the pre-X model Ks to present; and domestic singles and imports, the two-stroke tiddlers of 1947 through the Aermacchis of the late seventies. And we'll look at sources for parts and information.

A few words of warning: Some of the material in this book, such as bore and stroke and when a model was introduced, is a matter of record. Some of it is straight reporting—like model weights recorded by honest magazines on certified scales.

Some facts are firsthand; when I say you can use Sportster heads on an iron XR or an FX kick lever on a Sportster shaft, I say it because I did it. But some of the material here is opinions, recollections. Sometimes I got two answers to the same question. The experts interviewed are honest and experienced. They're also human, which is to say fallible. Their facts are subject to the influence of time and personal involvement.

There may be errors in this book. I know that. What I don't know is where they are.

The management folks at Harley-Davidson are understandably proud of their customers' devotion to the brand. What other company, they ask, inspires its fans to have the brand name tatooed on their arms?

Thus, Harley-Davidson is also protective of the various names and model descriptions used by, and copyrighted by, the company.

Let the record show, therefore, that Sportster, Electra Glide, Super Glide, Duo Glide, Harley-Davidson, H-D, Low Rider, Wide Glide, Tour Pak, Fat Bob, Roadster, Softail and any other Harley names, including the one word Harley itself, and emblems or designations in this book are the property of the Harley-Davidson Motor Company, Inc.

Next, money.

We are in relative good luck. The car enthusiasts have a problem. Cars have mass social appeal and rare cars give their owners a big boost in public. This has caused the prices of exotic cars, Ferraris, for example, to escalate to the edge of obscenity. There's so much money chasing a limited supply of such cars that a 1962 Ferrari 250GTO now sells for $300,000 and a 1957 Chevy may bring $20,000.

Motorcycles, though, lack trendiness. There's no mass appeal. The man on the street can't tell one from the other, so people who need ego magnification can't get it on two wheels.

This has kept prices on a human scale. The top-of-the-line Harley with all options sells for about $15,000. And if you have patience and a good poker face you can ride home on the finest old Harley, the rarest of the legends, for less than $15,000.

Your bike won't make you a fortune. Neither will it cost you a fortune. Fair, I think, because those who are in this hobby for anything except fun won't be here long, anyway.

There are some trends to keep in mind. One, depreciation. The current Harleys are terrific machines, the best the factory has ever made. This is good for business, but when you have improved new bikes for sale, the older models depreciate, something Harleys didn't used to do.

Two, nobody can really predict the future. We can carefully note what's going on now and we can expect whatever it is to continue, for a week or a month or a year. Keep in mind, though, that nobody expected OPEC or television.

Despite this, one can make educated guesses.

This book includes a rating system: This is, after all, a buyer's guide.

The system is based on stars, which indicate a predicted value or investment potential.

★★★★★ Five stars are the best, the top. A five-star model is one which either is or will become a special bike, one more people will want in the future, meaning the value will go up faster than the others.

★★★★ Four stars are also the models that will appreciate, except they may already have become desirable, or they may be a bit more risky, less of a sure thing.

★★★ Three stars are the average, the median. If you restore one you should be able to get out what you put in. Or if you buy a used one in good shape and ride it, when you sell you won't have lost much, and might even break even.

★★ Two stars are less than good investments. They're probably going to lose value, which is why you can get them cheap now.

★ One star is a sure loss. Nobody wants it; nobody wanted it when it was new. Walk away as politely as you can.

But remember, this is a guide. It may be educated but it's still mostly guesswork. Don't expect a five-star machine to make your fortune. Conversely, if you fall in love with a model that nobody wanted when new and which has no stars at all, ignore the experts. Listen to your heart and get the bike you like.

Concerning Specifications

The specifications used through this book were compiled with the help of shop manuals, owner manuals, history books, factory brochures and ads, and from tests conducted by the enthusiast magazines.

No one of the above sources directly compares with any other source. The factory generally tells the public what it wants the public to know, no more and no less. The public, in turn, was much less technically oriented in the past, while the mechanical details were less important: If the two competing models from the two factories had the same wheelbase, neither bothered to tell anybody what that wheelbase was.

In the early days the magazines were more inclined to praise than actually test, so they seldom weighed or clocked the bikes. And now that the magazines are honest and do perform their own measurements, each has its own system.

So we have some blanks and some confusion. The dry weights on the spec charts are usually the factory's claim and thus uncertified. *Cycle*, *Cycle World* and *Road Rider* use certified scales but their rules have varied over the years. Sometimes the bike is weighed empty, sometimes with full tanks and for years *Cycle World* used half a tank, on the reasonable fact that you can't ride a motorcycle with the tank really full or really empty.

Sometimes the factory claimed a power output, sometimes not. *Cycle* for years subjected test machines to dynamometer testing and reported the actual power measured. All this is fair and valid while not delivering the same scale over the more than fifty years reported here.

In sum, the charts are for information, but not for direct comparison.

Chapter 1

Big Twins

★★★★★	Knuckleheads 1936-47
★★★★	Panheads 1948-65
★★★★★	Shovelheads 1966-69
★★★★	Shovelheads 1970-80
★★★	Shovelheads 1981-84
★★★	V2 Evolution FLT, FLHT 1984-86

Exactly why Harley-Davidson introduced a radical new model in 1936 the history books don't say. Motorcycle sales in the early thirties were even worse than sales in general. Motorcycle enthusiasm was at an all-time low, with only about 100,000 machines registered in the US. The lone surviving motorcycle magazine had but a handful of readers.

Harley was the dominant force in what market there was, well ahead of arch rival Indian. The two makes offered similar models: side valve V-twins in 45, 74 or 80 cu. in. displacements. The Indian 45 was faster and more sporting than the Harley 45, while the Harley 74 had the legs on the Indian 74, so there was parity of a sort.

Heck of a time to rock the boat but in the spring of 1936, that's just what Harley did.

The engine and the model it powered bore the name E. The E had the classic H-D configuration of V-twin with included angle of 45° and the familiar dimensions of 3.31 in. bore and 3.5 in. stroke for a displacement of 61 cu. in., same as the Harley J models had in the twenties.

But while the other Harleys and the Indians were side valve and the earlier 61 cu. in. Harley had overhead (ohv) intake and side exhaust, the 61E had both sets of valves in the heads. This wasn't a new idea; Harley, Indian and about a dozen other makes had ohv racers, some with four valves per cylinder and others with overhead camshafts, on their racing engines back in the teens. But such systems were noisy and expensive to build and required lots of maintenance. Side valves, flatheads in the slang of that and later days, became the standard for road machines, motorcycles and cars. (Indeed, Ford and Plymouth used flathead engines well into the fifties.)

Knuckleheads: E, EL, F and FL, 1936-47

Because the 61E was the ancestor of all Harley's present engines, it's worth a detailed look.

First, how it looked. Most motorcycle engines of that time used a series of camshafts, a row of short shafts with one lobe each, geared together and each lobe working one valve. The E motor had one longer shaft with four lobes. It was mounted outboard of the crankshaft—except Harley doesn't use that term (we'll see why shortly)—and the camshaft's four lobes worked pushrods angled up tubes to the cylinder heads. Atop the heads were rocker arms, pivoting toward the center of the vee for the intakes, outboard for the exhausts. The intake ports and carburetor were naturally in the center of the vee and the exhaust ports and pipes were at the outer corners. The rockers, shafts, valve stems and springs were covered, the better to preserve the oil supply.

The E's rocker covers look special today. They didn't look so in 1936. If you look at a 1936 Vincent or an air-cooled aircraft engine from back then, you'd see the same general layout of covered pushrods, finned barrels and closely fitted rocker covers.

But that's technology. For folklore, hold up your hand, palm facing out. Make a fist. Notice the row of knuckles? Viewed from the right side (the rider's right when astride), the Harley E motor looks like a fist with protruding knuckles. From that look, and because people like nicknames, the E became and still is known as the Knucklehead.

Next, Harleys didn't have crankshafts because the factory terminology didn't admit to them. Instead, they had paired flywheels, one left and one right. The flywheels were big plates with holes in their centers for the drive shaft (left) or the pinion shaft (right). Each flywheel had a second hole outboard of the center by half the length of the stroke, that is, an engine with a 4 in. stroke had this hole two inches from the center. These flywheels were assembled by putting between them a crankpin fitted into each outer hole. The connecting rods, slip-fitted in a (blush) male-female relationship, were on this crankpin. The drive and pinion shafts faced outward and ran in bearings pressed into the left and right halves of the crankcase, which naturally bolted together. The left shaft turned the engine sprocket in the primary case on the left; the right shaft turned the gears for the camshaft, the ignition timer (Harleys didn't have distributors, either), the generator and the oil pump.

The Knucklehead engine was very much an assembly of parts. The ignition timer looked kind of like a car's fuel pump. It sat on

The grandfather; in this case a 1936 EL owned and restored by Armando Magri, Sacramento's dean of Harley dealers.

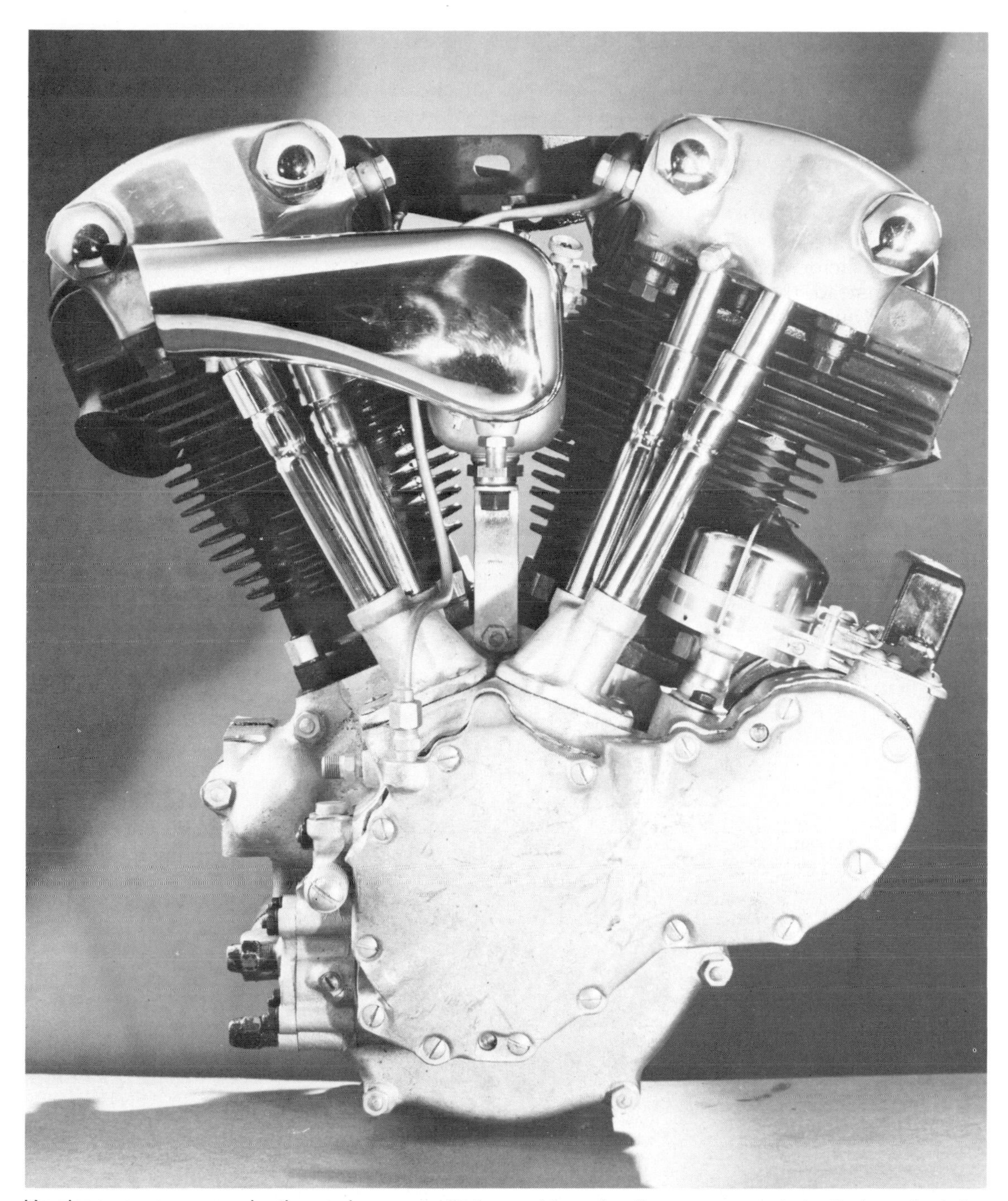

Up close you can see why the engine was called the Knucklehead. The camshaft was behind the cover, the pushrods were inside the angled tubes and the chromed object to the right of the front pushrods was the ignition timer. The generator, driven by the same geartrain that worked the camshaft and the timer, bolted to the timing case and rode below the front cylinder. The air horn in the center of the vee fed the carburetor, nestled in the top of the vee. Harley-Davidson photo.

top of the timing cover, just below the carburetor. The timer had a set of points operated by a two-lobe camshaft and timed in sequence with the V-twin's irregular firing order. There was one lead from this timer to a coil with two secondary wires, one to each spark plug. Each time the points broke, a spark went to both plugs. This didn't do the harm you might think because the wasted spark arrived when that cylinder was at the end of its exhaust stroke so there was nothing there to be ignited. All it really meant in daily service was that you never needed worry about which plug wire went on which plug. Either would do on either.

The timing case extended to in front of and below the front cylinder, where the generator was mounted, driven by a train of gears. The E's electrics were 6 volt, as was everything back then. The oil pump attached at the lower rear of the timing case and pulled oil from the separate tank and pushed oil back into the tank. It was a dry sump in technical terms but not in real life, as we'll see.

The primary case bolted to the left side of the crankcase and contained the engine sprocket, with a chain between it and the clutch sprocket. The gearbox bolted to the frame and fit on the primary case but it wasn't permanent: The primary chain was adjusted by moving the gearbox back and forth. (Here's a tip for novice Harley spotters: All big twins have their final drive, whether chain or belt, on the left. All Sportsters, some of which look like bigger twins in later years, have their final drive chains on the right.)

Perhaps the major technical leap for the E engine was its oil system. Earlier Harleys, in fact most motorcycles of the time and

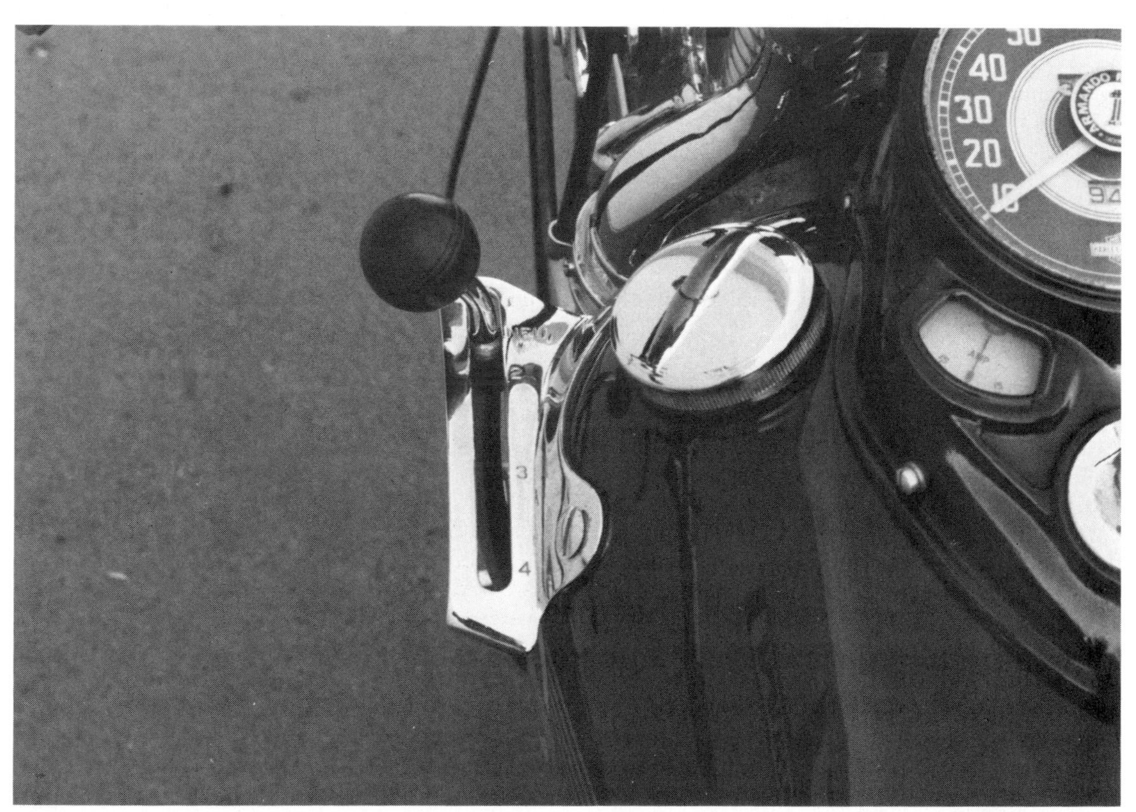

Hand shift had first all the way forward, then neutral, second, third and fourth, moving back. The instruments were housed in a panel between the two fuel tanks.

earlier, used what was known as the total loss system—the rider pumped oil from a tank into the engine, and it ran around inside and sort of dribbled out. Not only had the ecology craze not been invented, pavement was rare and engines burned so much oil anyway it didn't make any difference.

But the E engine had the double pump and separate tank, a dry sump in technical terms. Further, a single or a twin had wide fluctuations in crankcase pressure. When the pistons came down the cylinders, pressure went up; when they went up, pressure dropped. This was handled in Harley engines by a timed breather, a rotating valve that opened and closed so the pressure didn't get too high or too low. The engineers took advantage of this with the E by having the crankcase vacuum pull the oil back from the cylinder heads into the crankcase, which led to later problems (which we'll discuss in due course).

The E engine was housed in a double cradle, two tubes running from the steering head down and below the engine. That was another advance, in that previous Harleys used one tube, like the bicycle from which the motorcycle grew. Frame shape was still like a bicycle—a parallelogram formed by horizontal tubes between seat and steering head and between the rear hub and what used to be the crank and pedals. An angled tube ran from steering head to crank and another went from the seat to the rear hub. The shape was that of a diamond, and the proper name was diamond frame. This diamond was bisected by a downtube, from seat to crank, so the frame was two triangles, nature's strongest shape. The forward triangle had its vee at the bottom, which made it the perfect place to install a V-twin engine. It's fair to say the classic V-twin was made to fit those early frames, rather than the other way around.

Also like those pioneer bicycles, the E had no rear suspension. The rear wheel hub and brake were solidly bolted to the frame. The 61E was thus rigid, a hardtail in later parlance. Historically, this is odd. Some factories, Indian for one, used rear suspension back in 1912. But it didn't work very well and the idea fell from favor, so rear suspension didn't become common until the thirties and wasn't universal until the fifties.

Harley instead put the rider, and passenger in later years, on a seat that pivoted in front and was sprung and oil damped via springs and a sliding pillar. The rear wheel may have thud into a pothole but the rider was isolated from the shock. It worked better than one might think, which is why it lasted so long.

Front suspension was provided from 1907 on. The E model used forks consisting of two pairs of articulated struts. The rear pair was attached solidly to the steering stem and clamps. At the lower end was a pair of links, leading forward to the axle and the second pair of struts. The forward pair moved up and down, not far but far enough, via links to the rear pair, controlled by springs between them.

These springer forks also worked better than a modern rider would expect. Harley used this design from 1907 until 1949 and during the interim licensed other factories to use the design, proof that the system was a good one.

The E's gears, four forward speeds, were selected by hand with a lever moving back and forth in a gate on the left side of the fuel tank. The clutch control was a pedal, in front of the left floorboard. It had a friction disc so the pedal stayed where you left it, unlike car clutches that come up when the foot is removed. (A popular modification at one time, for reasons unknown, was a clutch that worked like a car clutch, so if you suddenly needed to use your left foot for balance and the bike was in gear, out came the clutch and away you went. This was known as a "suicide clutch" for obvious reasons.)

The hand shift and foot clutch were standard on motorcycles then, and had been since the beginning. First, that's how cars did it. Second, the practical foot-select gearshift had to wait for the invention of the positive stop shift drum, which gets to the next gear and waits there until pressure is released.

The 61E used two fuel tanks, slung on each side of the frame backbone. The new model had a valve so the rider could use the main or reserve tank. Previously the rider could switch from the first tank to the second but then had to guess how much was left. The reserve setting was less apt to make one walk.

Now we begin deciphering Harley's complicated code. The factory used the letters A, B and C to designate singles made about this time; D was for an earlier twin. So E came in the normal sequence.

Next, the E engine was the baseline model. The sporting version was the EL, with higher compression ratio and a larger intake manifold. But why L stood for higher compression, nobody remembers. (There was a third version, the ES, which came with lower gearing for sidecar use. S obviously meant sidecar.)

That first 61E had some teething troubles. The valve gear didn't work right and the factory had to ship fix kits quickly. Later the frame proved to be too light (so light that it broke) and the rear brake was weak. Still later there was a more permanent fix for the valve gear leaks, in the shape of larger rocker covers, part of the changes for the 1938 models.

None of these problems mattered much. The 61 was a hit; never mind that the old-timers grumbled that the JD series had been better. The 61 was fast and sporting, up to date in every way. A superbike, we'd say now, with lots of appeal for the big-spending road burners. Alas, there weren't many of them, not in the depressed thirties, but they estab-

Here you can see the sliding post for the seat, the floorboards, the brake pedal and Magri's smaller and more sporting air horn.

lished a reputation that may still be with us. Marlon Brando and that 1953 movie may have reinforced the image of motorcyclists as crazies, but they didn't invent it. (Nor did Brando ride a Harley in *The Wild One*. It was a Triumph.)

Details. The 1936 model 61 had no detents on the gate, which made shifting touchy. That, the frame and the rear brake were fixed for 1937. Oddly, the 1939 model had neutral between second and third rather than between first and second, for no reason shown in the books. Other than minor details, though, the Knuckleheads were pretty much alike for their first five years.

Harley updated the flathead 74 and enlarged it to 80 cu. in., meanwhile, and changed the name from V to U. But by 1941 it was clearly wasteful to make two engines so close in output and so different in design. So the U was dropped in favor of a Knucklehead engine with larger bore and stroke. Displacement became 74 cu. in. and, keeping with tradition, the names were F, FL and FS.

About this time World War II was heating up and the factory was busy making motorcycles for the military. After the war, pent-up demand kept the old design saleable, so except for minor changes in wheels, compression ratios and so on, the Knuckleheads in E and F sizes remained in production until 1947.

What to look for

First, the bad news. You aren't going to wander into a dusty barn and stumble over a perfectly preserved Knucklehead. We've all been hoping to do that for twenty years and all the barns have been wandered through.

Instead, there are restored examples, some of which come up for sale, at an asking price of $6,000, maybe $7,000 if it's really nice. (What they get isn't always what they ask, but true selling price is hard to learn.)

Or a local shop will have a chopper, probably badly done, with a Knucklehead engine. You maybe can save the frame. Most of the other major parts are around, in used form as found, or in reproduction parts, sometimes better than new.

For reference, in those apparently simpler days, the factory used its code as its code; that is, the left crankcase half had 39EL or perhaps 47FL stamped at the first part of the serial number. The rest of the engine may not actually be the year and size and tune the letters signify, but it's a beginning. If you're going to restore a 1938 61E, of course, the engine better have the correct letters.

Most parts are easy. Trim and minor hardware can be harder to find, especially if

A used Knuckle head. The rockers pivoted on shafts that mounted on the lugs sticking out of the fins.

Underside of the Knuckle head. Barely visible is a crack in the exhaust port, on the left. It can be fixed, which is good because these heads are rare and thus expensive.

you insist on factory originals. The least available big parts are the heads, although a good mechanic can repair what look like hopeless examples, right down to new valve seats and new threads for the intake manifold. Cylinders are often tired—heck, who wouldn't be after nearly fifty years? The practical solution here is to use stronger, more easily located barrels from the Panhead engines.

However, the inclusion of crankcase vacuum in the oiling system design means that all seals and joints and connections must be perfect. Often they aren't, and Knuckleheads are famous leakers and dribblers. The top repair shops say it can be done, but be ready to learn how, or pay for the skill.

Rating: Five full stars

The value of these machines (the year doesn't matter much) is established and rising. Even so, a good one is a best buy. They're rare, which doesn't hurt. They look wonderful, a treat for the eye.

Magri's Knucklehead has been painstakingly restored. Things Harley no longer provides are the rear stand, hinged rear fender for easy wheel removal and a toolbox, the black box (funny words), on the rear frame tubes between the hub and the kick-start lever.

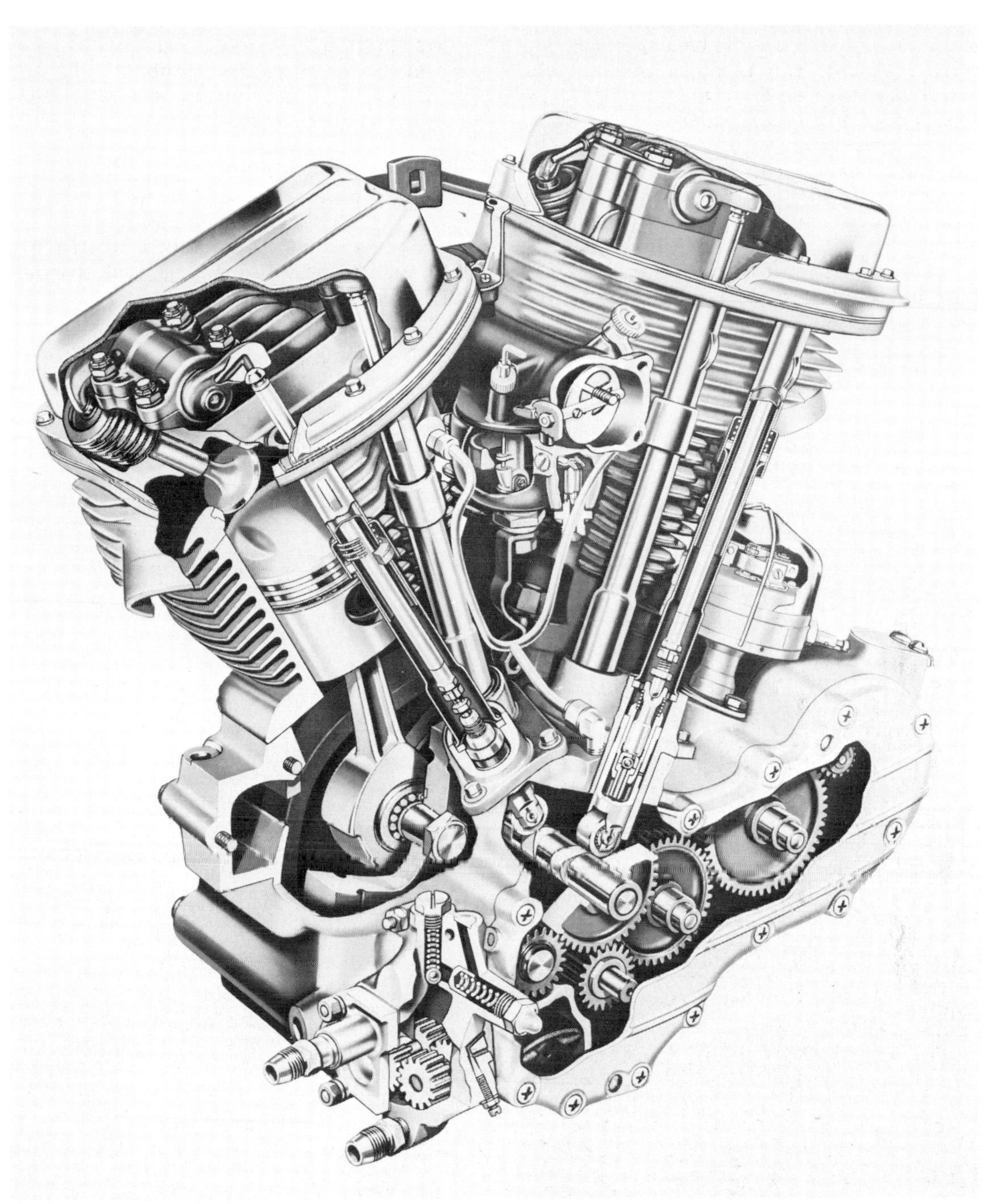

Cutaway of the later Panhead engine shows the valve lifters in their housings atop the timing case, the system of pushrods and rocker arms, and the outside oil lines. Note how much this engine is otherwise like the Knucklehead. Harley-Davidson photo.

And they're a good machine for the ordinary collector. If you go all out with time and money the result can win best of show, or at least best in class. If you aren't quite as fussy, you can build a reasonably authentic example, perhaps with better lights and seat, and you've got a machine you can show with pride and also actually ride on nice Sunday afternoons.

Year and model	1936 E (Knucklehead)
Engine	ohv 45° V-twin
Bore and stroke	3.31x3.5 in.
Displacement	61 cu. in.
BHP	40 (claimed)
Gearbox	4 speeds
Shift	left hand
Wheelbase	59.5 in.
Wheels	18 in. (later 16)
Suspension	springer forks, rigid rear
Weight	565 lb. (dry)
Seat height	n/a
MPG	n/a
Top speed	90 mph (claimed)

Panheads: EL, FL and FLH, 1948-65

Nostalgia comes only with hindsight and the Harley engineers weren't being unreasonable when they improved on the now-legendary Knucklehead, which they did for the 1948 model year. There were some natural parallels with the car companies, in that most American factories did war work during the war while thinking about what to do when peace broke out. Harley beat Ford and General Motors to postwar models by one year, albeit it didn't go as far with its changes.

The Knucklehead's main problems had been oil control and oil consumption. The basic package, as in the lower end, clutch, gearbox and so forth, was sound. So the engineers kept all that as it was and introduced a new top end for the engine.

Barrels and cylinder heads were new. The barrels were still cast iron but the heads were aluminum alloy, lighter and cooler than iron. Oil lines and passages were internal, to keep things cleaner. The oil pump was enlarged and the engine no longer used negative crankcase pressure to bring oil back to the tank.

The major technical change, aside from the use of alloy, involved the valve lifters. Again beating GM by a year and Honda by a generation, the revised E and F engines used hollow valve lifters. These cavities were filled with oil and maintained the needed clearance in the valvetrain without having to set that clearance mechanically.

Car engines adopted this principle in the early fifties, while motorcycles stuck with solid lifters, feeler gauges and wrenches until a few years ago, when Honda discovered the idea and made a big fuss about it.

The lifters originally went at the top of the pushrod tubes, between pushrod and rocker arm, but in 1953 they were moved to between cam lobe and pushrod, atop the timing case.

The engine's major visible change was the rocker covers. The rockers were still mounted on the head, but instead of being covered closely, the heads were topped by covers over everything and held in place by a metal ring and a series of bolts around the perimeter. The covers looked like baking pans. Thus the engine quickly acquired the nickname, Panhead, also retained to this day.

As usual, early examples had some problems, in the form of leaks. Some of this was owner related. The covers had felt pads glued to their tops, used to absorb surplus oil and drip it back into circulation, and to keep the noise down. If these pads came loose, which they sometimes did, or if the owners left them out, the engine made a racket and didn't get the right amount of oil at the right time.

The hydraulic valve lifters would sometimes collapse and give too much clearance, or would stick at full extension and not give enough. And there was a joke about how you couldn't blow up a Panhead for lack of oil because if the oil level got too low the lifters would collapse and the engine wouldn't run.

Never mind. The lifters and the revised oil system worked better than the old way, provided the oil was changed on schedule and thus kept clean.

The rest of the engine was mostly the same, with the ignition timer running off the camshaft at right front and the generator in front of the forward cylinder. Still foot clutch and hand shift, although the pattern was reversed: First gear was at the back of the gate, and fourth was in front.

It's worth remembering here that the new top end went on both the 61, the E and EL, and the 74 cu. in. F and FL. Thus, while most people think of the Knucklehead as a 61 and the Panhead as a 74, there are 61 Pans and 74 Knuckles. Check the case letters and flywheels to be sure.

In a sense the 1948 Panhead was a top end swap, with the same basic engine in the previous frame. There was a new seat and minor stuff but the rear wheel was still rigid and the forks were still springers.

That changed in 1949, with the introduction of telescopic forks (same principle as used by nearly all motorcycles today). This was a big improvement, simply because the wheel could travel farther so the springs could be softer and the ride better.

There were teething problems, as the forks had been given a vent that sometimes blew oil onto the rider, but that, too, was taken care of quickly.

The other new part was a name. Until 1949, all Harleys went by letter or number, as in EL, WD, JD, or by nickname in the case of Panhead. But with the new forks came a model name, Hydra-Glide (always with a hyphen, just like Harley-Davidson).

There was also the beginning of a style trend. The Hydra-Glide was a substantial machine, with big, fat tires and fully valanced fenders and covers over the fork tubes. It was a part of its time—look at a 1949 Buick, for instance—but still a trend.

The next big step was in 1952. There was lots of other news that year, but the big twin headline was foot shift and hand clutch.

Not everyone switched, though. There were too many traditional buyers for that. But the 74 could be ordered as the FL, hand shift, or the FLF, foot shift. Because the clutch springs were designed for control by leg, which is stronger than arm, the hand control got a helper spring that went overcenter so it pulled with the rider when the springs got compressed. The standard gearbox was still four speeds forward, although for sidecar use three speeds forward and one reverse could be ordered until 1980.

Duo-Glide shared front end, engine and highway package options with the Hydra-Glide, but frame aft of seat was reworked to mount dual shocks, with swing arm pivoted behind the gearbox. Harley-Davidson photo.

1955 FLH, with the sprung dual saddle, windshield and leather saddlebags of the period. Luggage rack and the chromed guards everyplace were also popular.

Motorcycle magazines in those days weren't famous for being critical, but they did print the factory's specifications, something the factory's ads didn't always do, and they did have stopwatches. So we know now that a 1952 Hydra-Glide weighed about 600 lb., had a seat height of 31 in. and would do an honest 100 mph.

Also worth noting, the magazine testers of that time took all the bikes off pavement as a matter of course. All motorcycles then were expected to perform on dirt roads, and they did. How this worked, I don't know, but all Harleys through the FLH era were good on graded dirt or gravel while their modern rivals were not.

For 1952, the 61E was dropped from the line-up. The two versions of the same engine looked alike. The 74 was more powerful than the 61, but the 61 was smoother. Harley came out with a new line of smaller machines in 1952, and the price difference between the 61 and the 74 was only about $15, so the 61 was discontinued.

There were some small changes in 1953, such as medallions to celebrate the company's fiftieth anniversary. Also, the valve

Another dresser, this time a 1962 FLH with different seat and plastic bags. Serrated exhaust pipes fed one muffler.

lifters were moved from the heads to the timing case. Not much happened in 1954.

It's worth noting here that all during the fifty years spanned by this book, Harley-Davidson displayed an admirable sense of caution; the rate of change was deliberate. Harley installed a new engine in an old frame, for example, and a year or so after that the proven engine got a new frame or suspension.

Thus, the early Panhead remained static while the new suspension and different shifting system was put into production.

In 1955 Harley put a new bottom end underneath the heads and barrels. It didn't look much different; all the components were in the same places, but the main bearings were stronger and the cases changed, for the new bearings and a few other modifications.

The original E and F, the plain-Jane low-compression versions of the engine, had faded away and the FL had become the standard. With the stronger lower end, the engineers could tune the engine for more power, so the top of the 1955 line was the FLH.

One would have to guess that H stood for higher. The factory never explains why it picks names and letters. I mention this here because owners of the big twins used to outfit them with leather saddlebags and canvas windshields, from the factory and from outside suppliers. Leather and fabric became fiberglass and plastic, and bikes with all accessories became known as "dressers," as in fully dressed. Later the factory offered stock motorcycles with all these options already installed and the FLH is sometimes reported to stand for the highway version of the FL. But it doesn't.

The next big step, in 1958, was rear suspension. This was entirely logical. Harley already had a model with swing arm and dual spring/shock absorbers, and so did the other makers. This fully suspended model, still with Panhead engine in FL or FLH form,

Factory sketch of 1964 Duo-Glide shows lots of detail: stock, short seat; tool box in front of the rear shock; frame tubes at the upper shock mount; serrated exhaust covers; and, most of all, covers and nacelle for the fork tubes and headlight. Harley-Davidson photo.

became the Duo-Glide—glides at both ends, get it?

Again the factory built the same basic model for a few years, with changes like putting oil lines back on the outside of the engine, and changing wheel sizes and trim.

Then Honda arrived in 1959 and began meeting nice people, which enlarged the market for motorcycles. The Harley folks had never considered expanding the market, I suppose, because nobody had ever done it before. One of the ways Honda and the other Japanese factories enlarged the pie, as they say, was with electrical starting.

It made sense. So in 1965, taking a radical step, Harley came out with an electric leg for the 74. The electrical system was changed from 6 to 12 volts, a much larger battery was installed and the starter motor was mounted aft of the cylinders, where it could crank the engine through the primary drive.

The new model was named Electra Glide (originally with a hyphen, since abandoned).

There were some objections from purists who said (correctly) that if the engine was in good tune, it wasn't difficult to start with a few well-delivered kicks. Which it wasn't. *If* the engine was in good tune and *if* you had the skill and weight to deliver those kicks. In other words, the electric leg is nice to have. (A kick lever for back-up is also nice to have, but we'll get to that later.)

Those early electric starters gave trouble, but once more they were replaced and are all gone by now. Harleys used to come with toolboxes, on the right side of the frame. But the swing arm suspension and then the larger battery crowded the toolbox out, never to return, just as the rear stand was taken off but not replaced with the center stand most other motorcycles have.

Once all that was done—meaning the changes in suspension, shifting and starting, and introducing the stronger lower end—the factory lifted another foot from the ground and took the Panhead out of production at the end of 1965.

What to look for

Panhead-powered big twins have more differences than any of the Harleys made in our times. Thus there are lots of choices, in the book, anyway.

Massive battery on this 1965 Electra Glide has displaced the toolbox. This is a beautifully restored example; I don't believe the timing case cover or rear fender brackets were quite that shiny when new.

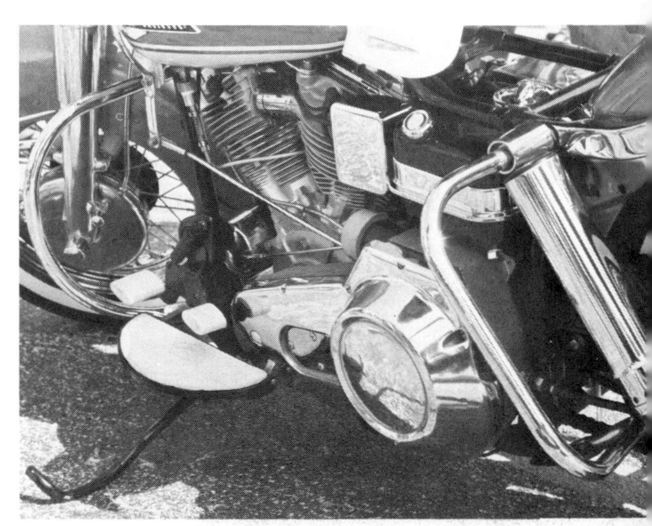

Left side of this 1965 FL shows polish, the revised primary cover for the electric start and what had become an option by then: hand shift and rocker clutch pedal.

In real life the Panhead era was also the beginning of the chopper era. Perhaps because some enthusiasts were putting on things like saddlebags and windshields, other enthusiasts began taking things off, or chopping them off, which is where the name came from. They chopped or removed the fenders, threw away the big tanks and used tiny tanks from scooters, moved the gear lever from the gate on the tank to a shorter lever below the seat. (The name for that is a jockey shift, by the way.) This was done to new and used machines and the Panheads, especially the early ones, were the machines most available, so a lot of them fell victim to this fashion.

So first, an original, untouched Panhead isn't easy to locate; when you do, the owner knows its value.

The parts curve goes up and down. There's such a demand for springer forks that people make them new—good ones. You can buy new reproductions, or you can hunt up leftover factory parts, known in the trade as NOS (new old stock), of the early and late cases and the cylinders.

In contrast, the official portrait of the 1965 Electra Glide has optional left-side muffler for the rear cylinder, foot lever for the gearshift and hand lever for the clutch. Saddlebags, rack, riding lights, fender trim and case guards were also options. Harley-Davidson photo.

The first thing to do is identify what's being offered. The factory used an easy system: The first numbers are the year and the first letters the model, as in 52FL or 59FLH. Obviously, if the engine says 54FL and the frame has a swing arm and shocks, somebody has made some swaps. That's not always wrong or bad. But if you want a completely stock motorcycle, check first.

Further, although all the engines will bolt into any frame, not all the engine parts can be assembled into a working engine. Each year's engine has something different about it. Some parts interchange and some don't, and you can't make the set unless you know what all the parts are.

Nobody (to my knowledge) is making new heads. They can be bought used and repaired. The hardest to find are the early ones, so take care if you decide on an early example.

Frames often lack numbers, but the rigid model is easily identified, as is the springer/telescopic variety. There were two versions of the Hydra-Glide frame: 1948 through early 1954 with bowed front downtubes, and late 1954 through 1957 with straight front tubes. The later frames are harder to find and thus priced higher.

Cheer up, though, if you want to have a bike to ride rather than a show bike, because all the engines, gearboxes, cycle parts and so on can be fixed and modified to work.

The hold-down rings for the valve covers were thin and sometimes the holes pushed their way through. You might consider using accessory covers, cast ones. They can be found and because they were so popular back then, it's a period modification nobody will hold against you.

Another useful change is to switch the 6-volt system to 12 volts, for better lights, switches and generator. The kick-start engines don't need a big battery so a small 12-volt battery can be hidden by the oil tank.

Year and model	1952 FL (Hydra-Glide)
Engine	ohv 45° V-twin
Bore and stroke	3.43x3.96 in.
Displacement	74 cu. in.
BHP	55 (claimed)
Gearbox	4 speeds
Shift	left foot
Wheelbase	60.5 in.
Wheels	16 in.
Suspension	telescopic forks, rigid rear
Weight	598 lb. (curb)
Seat height	31 in.
MPG	38
Top speed	102 mph

Year and model	1965 FLH (Electra Glide)
Engine	ohv 45° V-twin
Bore and stroke	3.43x3.96 in.
Displacement	74 cu. in.
BHP	60 (claimed)
Gearbox	4 speeds
Shift	left foot
Wheelbase	60 in.
Wheels	16 in.
Suspension	telescopic forks, swing-arm rear
Weight	783 lb. (curb)
Seat height	31.3 in.
MPG	n/a
Top speed	98 mph

Rating: Four careful stars

All this is public knowledge. The Panhead is a good engine, not overstressed and visibly different. The models span three eras and any of them can be used by ordinary people.

But everybody knows this. The Panhead market has already risen. (As a collector note, here and for other models, machines made for collection, like the ones with fiftieth anniversary medallions, don't acquire extra value, I suspect because everybody knows they're supposed to.)

Stock unrestored Panheads do still pop up in the classified ads, generally at reasonable, albeit constantly rising, asking prices. A show-worthy restoration will go for twice the price of a tired example kept running with parts from other models (be prepared also to spend more money maintaining the unrestored example.)

As a group, because the Panheads' values are established and known, the rating will be four stars—worth having but not worth putting your firstborn in hock.

Shovelheads: FL, FLH and FLT, 1966-84

In 1966, Harley-Davidson was keeping pace with the world. As described elsewhere,

Harley offered a full range of models, from single-cylinder sports machines to the FLH with highway package.

Call it evolution, a word we'll see again. But the engine that began as the sporting middleweight 61 had grown into the heavyweight 74, the biggest motorcycle on the market.

Because of this, the engine was working harder. And because of that, the factory came out with a new top end, third in the series.

The cylinder heads were topped not by rocker covers but by rocker boxes; the rocker arms pivoted on shafts attached to castings that bolted to the heads. Given some imagination, these castings looked like the back end of a coal shovel, so the new engine acquired its nickname, Shovelhead. The heads were still aluminum and barrels still iron, so the new heads retained the exterior oil lines returned to use on the late Panheads.

The FLH engine was rated at 60 bhp, the seldom-seen but still available FL at 54. The word rating is used here because those who owned both versions say the last Panheads were faster than the first Shovelheads, by ten or so miles per hour.

The new engine probably did have more power, while the new machine was slower. Electric starting added things like the starter motor itself, a bigger battery, extra wiring, additions estimated then at 75 lb.

Cycle World tested an FLH in 1967 and reported a curb weight of 783 lb. and a top speed of 98 mph. This test was done with full tanks, while previous reports had simply given the factory's claimed dry weight. But even so, the big twin had gained about 100 lb. in the model change while the earlier 74s and 61s had held their weight down for thirty years.

Allowing for the magazine's increased sophistication or perhaps its willingness to criticize, something the other magazines then were reluctant to do, *Cycle World* found a machine that did its job. It was a good highway bike, once one allowed for the sheer size of the thing. Not much was said about shake and vibration but in that day all motorcycles vibrated, so nobody noticed.

Other than the new heads, the early Shovelhead was a lot like its predecessor, as both had the ignition timer running out of the timing case and the generator on the front of

This 1967 FLH is a fine example of the dresser—bags and small top box, windshield, buddy seat with helper springs.

The present owner of this 1966 FL says it's a police model (see helmet). Plastic bags and stepped seat are standard modifications. Note ignition timer and shape of timing case.

the engine case. The early Shovels and late Pans were so much alike that today it's not unusual to see the top of one on the bottom of the other.

That and the factory's use of sometimes complicated identification systems can get confusing. Until 1970 the engines had type and year codes, while in 1965 the big twins acquired another letter, B, presumably for electric start. And the choice of hand or foot shift was still on the books. Thus, the full names were FLHFB, FLHB, FLFB and FLB; F for foot shift, H for higher compression, B (one assumes) for bigger battery.

This system lasted through 1969. In 1970 the B was dropped, perhaps because the back-up kick start had been deleted, and the system of designating the year of manufacture was changed to a letter for the decade and a number for the year—as in HO, meaning 1970. Through 1972 there were the FLHF, FLH, FLPF and FLP, the lower-compression FL having become the police model. In 1973 they reverted to the FLH and FL; in 1974 and 1975 it was the FLH-1200, FLHF and FL—enough variation here to make testing impossible. Not only could you and I not pass the quiz, I doubt if even the factory guys could. The men there now say there used to be a man in the plant who remembered everything, but he's retired.

For our purposes, there was the customer model, the FLH, and the FL, for police and escort work, and options of hand shift and reverse gear for eccentrics or sidecarists.

Through all this were mechanical changes, too. The kick starter disappeared and Harley invented the touring, or dresser, package. It was first seen in 1966, in the form

Long exhaust pipes on 1972 FLH dragged on driveways. *Road Rider* photo.

Disc front brake in 1972 was a real improvement. *Road Rider* photo.

Front view of 1974 FLH with bar-mount fairing. *Road Rider* photo.

of a windshield and saddlebags; actually they were rigid boxes on each side of the rear fender but the saddlebag name works so well it's still in use. The parent company had expanded into golf carts and various things using fiberglass, so Harley acquired a fiberglass company. The 1969 FLH had a fairing, mounted on the handlebars, with a painted body and clear screen. It enclosed the headlight, turned with the front wheel and set a style that lasted twenty-five years. The full touring option included the fairing, the saddlebags (called Pak-King) and a third case, on a rack above the rear fender, called Tour-Pak by Harley and a top box by everybody else.

The engine changed a lot for 1970. The cases were modified because the ignition timer was taken off the outside and became points in the timing case, while the generator in front was swapped for an alternator, inside the primary case. The timing case cover had a noticeable cone shape, so early engines are usually called Generator Shovels and later ones are Alternator Shovels or cone motors. The serrated exhaust pipe covers disappeared, which was just as well because the Shovel's single bolt holding pipe to exhaust port often comes loose.

Road Rider magazine tested a 1970 Electra Glide and liked it, for the most part. The oil tank now had a dipstick, while older bikes had the tank hidden under the seat, but the alternator widened the engine and moved the floorboards outboard, where they could more easily be dragged on the ground. The test bike had some wiring problems; one valve lifter collapsed but cured itself on the way to the shop, and the test bike got into a weave at 95 mph but straightened itself out if the rider powered through the trouble speed. Alas, *Road Rider* didn't do technical analysis or timed runs in those days so we don't know how fast the bike actually went. (There were complaints about the Tillotson carb fitted then, but in 1971 the factory switched to a Bendix, which also got cussed. Later standard wear is a Keihin, which can have problems, too.)

Road Rider's 1972 FLH had a disc front brake, which stopped the bike with too little effort, the magazine said, and that was the last time anybody said that about a Harley. The magazine's test bike dragged the muffler

They didn't have throttle return springs in 1974. This FLH is a median example, with fairing and bags, but also with solo seat and rack. *Road Rider* photo.

tips on driveways, had trouble with the Bendix carb and got 39 mpg, the only measured result published.

Cycle World did a test of the 1973 Electra Glide with King of the Road package, which included windshield, spotlights, case guards front and rear, saddlebags, chrome trim to protect the bags, a leather tool pouch and the famous sprung saddle, now long enough to be a comfortable fit for two people.

This 1973 FLH weighed 738 lb. with 5 gal. tanks half full. Wheelbase was 61.4 in., seat height was 34 in., the engine was rated at 66 bhp. The test bike returned 37 mpg, did 0-60 mph in 7.6 sec., the standing quarter mile in 15.42 sec. with a trap speed of 84 mph and stopped from 60 mph in 168 ft.

The magazine called the FLH "A remnant from a past era." What it meant was that the Electra Glide or 74 or FLH, the names interchanged, had become a distinctly different motorcycle from the rest of the models on the market. There was no toolbox, no center stand, no kick lever. The turn signals blinked as long as you held down the buttons. The side stand locked in place, but there was no lock for the steering head. The throttle had no return spring. The shift lever had two ends; it was a rocking lever so you pushed down with the heel to shift up, and down with the toe to shift down. The floorboards dragged on the ground during hard cornering and the engine vibrated so much it was hard to keep your boots on the boards.

In short, the booming motorcycle market had attracted other large models from other companies and these rivals didn't do what the FLH had always done, so the original had become different.

The company held fast. The Keihin carb arrived in 1974, along with a revised saddle and an alarm system. (Then, as now, Harley was the most popular motorcycle to steal.) The 1975 model carried over. In 1976 you could order insignia celebrating America's Bicentennial. The seat was changed again for 1977 and along with the choice of black or silver, the buyer could get one of a limited run of Classics, in brown with complementary tan trim.

The 1978 collector bike was the Special Edition 75th Anniversary (Harley's, not the USA's) Electra Glide. It came with black paint, gold trim and striping, real leather on the seat and a cast gold-looking anodized eagle on the clutch cover.

There were other, more important changes that year. For one, the ignition became electronic, as in breakerless, or CD, the dreaded black box.

Return of the 80

Second, the Shovelhead was enlarged, from 74 to 80 cu. in., by increasing bore and stroke. There was precedent, such as the old flathead V-twins from Indian and Harley.

Another 1974 74, with added radio, crash bars and trim. *Road Rider* photo.

Road Rider's 1977 test FLH was a starting point; no fairing, shield or saddlebags. *Road Rider* photo.

And there was reason. As we've noted, the FLH was a heavy machine. Government rules controlled emissions levels and pump gas wasn't what it used to be. So the Shovelhead 74 had been increasingly leaned, retarded, restricted. The easiest way to keep performance was to increase displacement.

So the engine grew to 80 cu. in. or 1340 cc. Compression ratio was 8:1 and claimed power was 65, about what it had been earlier

This gleaming 1977 Shovelhead engine illustrates the cone-shaped timing case cover used from 1970 through 1984. *Road Rider* photo.

Easiest way to distinguish the 80 cu. in. Shovelhead from the 74 version is the air cleaner. After that, count the fins on the barrel. Giant air cleaner was mandated by federal noise rules. *Road Rider* photo.

The 1977 FLH tested by *Road Rider*, after the addition of saddlebags, top box and fairing. *Road Rider* photo.

with the 74. The 80 didn't have more power, it had softer, quieter, cleaner power.

The 80 engine looked almost exactly like the 74. One quick way to tell was to count the fins on the cylinder. The 74 barrel had ten fins. Because the 80 barrel had a thicker base, allowing room for the nuts and bolts holding barrel to case, there was room for only nine fins.

The 80 was first offered in 1978 as the FLH-80, with black cherry paint, cast wheels, a new air cleaner and the new ignition all part of the package.

Cycle World's example weighed 752 lb. with the dual 5 gal. tanks half full. With fairing, bags and so on, the FLH-80 did the quarter mile in 15 sec. and topped out at 89 mph. The reporters found the foot brake and rocker shift pedal awkward to use but said the clutch was light. And the FLH-80 did its job; it was smooth and comfortable at 60-70 mph, normal cruising speed for most people when the coast is clear.

The special model became an option for all Electra Glides in model year 1979. There was also a Limited Edition Electra Glide, with paint in tan and creme (factory spelling, not mine) and with cast wheels, fairing, bags, top box and case guards all standard. The seat shown in the ads was mounted solidly to the

The 1978 FLH-80 looked just like the plain FLH of that year. The machine in background is a 1976 (I think—hard to see under all that trim) with an aftermarket fairing, larger than the factory's. *Road Rider* photo.

frame, although it did say the sprung seat could be ordered.

At mid-year 1979 the factory brought out a sidecar model, code name CLE. It had the 80 engine, 16 in. wheels front, back and side and the forks were more steeply raked so steering effort was less than it otherwise would have been. *Road Rider* borrowed one and had a good time, as sidecars can be fun if you allow for their quirks.

The CLE was geared lower to allow for the greater weight but still managed to get 36 mpg and 677 miles per quart (mpqt.) of oil. Oddly enough, the factory put the sidecar back into the catalog just about the time it deleted reverse gear. (Note here that because sidecars are so different and so rare, they are only mentioned in passing. Only a handful have been sold during the time we're reviewing so they have no effect on the survey.)

The Electra Glide range for 1980 was narrow. There was the Classic model, with the big top box and all extras, in tan and creme or charcoal and black, with the 80 engine standard. And there was the plain Electra Glide, with the 74 engine standard, the 80 optional and also with fairing, bags and rack but no top box.

The Tour Glide

The exciting 1980 news was a new model, the first for Harley-Davidson in

Year and model	1973 FLH (Electra Glide)
Engine	ohv 45° V-twin
Bore and stroke	3.43x3.96 in.
Displacement	74 cu. in.
BHP	66 (claimed)
Gearbox	4 speeds
Shift	left foot
Wheelbase	61.4 in.
Wheels	16 in.
Suspension	telescopic forks, swing-arm rear
Weight	738 lb., tank half full
Seat height	34 in.
MPG	37
Top speed	95 mph (observed)

Year and model	1978 FLH-80 (Electra Glide)
Engine	ohv 45° V-twin
Bore and stroke	3.50x4.25 in.
Displacement	82 cu. in.
BHP	65 (est.)
Gearbox	4 speeds
Shift	left foot
Wheelbase	61.5 in.
Wheels	16 in.
Suspension	telescopic forks, swing-arm rear
Weight	752 lb., tank half full
Seat height	31.4 in.
MPG	49
Top speed	89 mph

The rarest of charmers, a sidecar. This is the CLE, an FLH-80 with cast 16 in. wheels all around. *Road Rider* photo.

The CLE came with the tan and creme paint scheme used on the Classic FLH. Harleys have used sidecars for 60 or so years, but they drive (not ride) differently and have never been common, or cheap; this rig's price gets into five figures. *Road Rider* photo.

nearly ten years. The designation was FLT and the name was Tour Glide.

The name and designation may be misleading. The FLT used the 80 engine, the primary case and the gearbox all attached to each other as they'd been since 1936.

But there the similarity ends. The FLT was a different motorcycle altogether. It had a different frame. More important, the engine/primary case/transmission were bolted into one solid mass and the swing arm pivoted on that mass. The drivetrain was attached to the frame, and thus to the front suspension, hand grips, seat and floorboards, through the medium of flexible, compressible mounts. The mounts were made of miracle synthetic material, not rubber, although that's what people think of for shock- and vibration-absorbing mounts (and in fact people sometimes call this model the Rubber Glide.)

This three-point mounting system didn't cure or reduce shake and vibration. It isolated them from the rider, which amounts to the same thing.

The new frame extended in front of the steering head, so it was stiffer and served as a place to attach the permanent full fairing.

The front fork tubes were angled differently and placed behind the steering stem rather than in front of it, so at low speeds the FLT steered lighter than it was. The gearbox had a fifth speed, the drive chain was enclosed and lubricated by its own oil supply, the CD ignition was revised, there was a spin-on oil filter, bigger disc brakes, dual headlights, bigger saddlebags and top box, all standard as delivered. The frame didn't allow for the old sprung saddle and claimed dry weight was 725 lb., but those were the only debits.

At this point the compass needle begins to spin. In the FLT we have a really new and different model. Almost all it had in common with the 1966 FLH was a larger version of the Shovelhead engine.

So we interrupt this review of mechanical specifications to look at what else was happening at Harley-Davidson and why the company did what it did.

When the Japanese got serious about making and selling motorcycles they created a new kind of machine and a new kind of customer.

Harley-Davidson wasn't caught unawares, however. Harley began making small motorcycles at home in 1947 and bought an Italian company to supply lightweights for the US when the home-built products were priced out of the market in 1960.

But things still looked bleak. In 1965 and in 1966 the Harley and Davidson families offered shares in what had been a privately, or at least closely, held company. A bit less than half the shares went to outsiders and capital was raised.

It wasn't enough. The other motorcycle factories were bigger and moved faster. In 1969, after some corporate infighting not worth describing here, Harley-Davidson was bought by American Machine & Foundry, now known as AMF.

There are at least two sides to this story. The one you're most likely to hear is the one about how AMF nearly ruined Harley.

AMF is a big conglomerate and thus not likely to show sensitivity for individual feelings. For rational reasons most of Harley's operations were removed from their traditional Milwaukee home to York, Pennsylvania, where AMF had a suitable factory. Work was disrupted and workers lost work. There were hard feelings and reports of sabotage. There were some serious problems with quality control. So there are today Harley fans who sincerely believe AMF set out to gut the fine old firm, take the money and run.

This is neither fair nor accurate. AMF had grabbed more than it could handle. It takes a while to learn how to build things, especially complicated ones like motorcycles. And to train people and correct mistakes.

Next, the motorcycle boom was even stronger than anybody had dared predict. In 1965 Harley-Davidson's total production was 25,328, including twins and singles, imports and domestics. In 1970, the year AMF took effective control, the total was 28,850. And in 1975, Harley's all-time high, the total was 75,403.

While the new production lines were working at top speed, there were also more models than ever before. And there were more rules than ever before, so engineers were diverted from design and production into noise and emission control.

As still another factor, AMF was in business to do business, which isn't the same thing as being in business to make motorcycles. Like any corporate giant, the AMF rules were much less strict for approving capital expenditures than approving spending money on the product, never mind on the people or on research and development.

AMF invested literally millions of dollars in Harley-Davidson. Production facilities were improved beyond description. But while some thought was given to the future and a few new models appeared, the emphasis wasn't on the product.

And then the curve turned down: 61,375 bikes were built in 1976, 45,608 in 1977, 41,586 in 1981.

What happened, beyond the obvious? There was a recession. And the rival makers had moved in on Harley's market with big touring machines, and yes, people in general had lost interest in motorcycles once all the people who'd always wanted one had one.

Another pause here. In the middle of 1981 a new partnership was formed. Some of the members were of the founding families. Others were long-time Harley employees. And several came from AMF. This group arranged to borrow millions from the banks and buy Harley-Davidson back from AMF.

There was great rejoicing on both sides. AMF wanted to turn back to the industrial business, having had its fling with leisure-time pursuits. And the rate of return on investment wasn't what it had been.

The joy at Harley was even more direct. AMF had paid for the new plants and (I suspect here, no proof has turned up) saved Harley from bankruptcy. The new owners, having invested their careers, savings accounts and second mortgages, could improve the product.

And with that background behind us, we can get back to the FLT.

It was (and is) a better motorcycle than the FLH in almost every way. By designing the package as one integrated whole, with the drivetrain tailored to the frame and suspension, the frame ready to hold fairing, saddlebags and so forth, the FLT sidestepped all the compromises imposed during the FLH years.

So, for 1980, Harley offered the Electra Glide Classic. It came in black with charcoal and in tan and creme, all options and the 80 engine standard. There was the baseline Electra Glide, usually equipped with bags and fairing, either the 74 or the 80 Shovelhead, and the FLT.

Cycle World tested an FLT in 1980 and words nearly failed the writers. The big bike was stable and agile at the same time. It could be leaned around corners, the steering was light; better in every way, they marveled.

In the facts column, the FLT weighed 781 lb. with the 5 gal. tank half full. It did the standing quarter mile in 15.86 sec., gave 42 mpg and had a top speed of 91 mph (a shade slower overall than the FLH-80, which fig-

Tour Glide's frame-mounted fairing used dual headlights, and was wider and taller than the FLH barmount fairing. *Road Rider* photo.

ures considering the added weight and the size of the fairing). The testers didn't like the solid-mount seat as much as the old suspended saddle, but that was the only complaint.

The 74 cu. in. Shovelhead was dropped from the catalog in 1981 for the same reason the 61 bowed to the 74—not as much power for nearly the same amount of money. The FLT had the same paint and trim as the FLH and even carried the word Classic—meaning full-boat, no-extras-spared—on the front fender.

The 80 engine had a hidden improvement for 1981. Because the added displacement added power, and gas was lousy anyway, the 80's compression ratio was reduced from 8:1 to 7.4:1. This let it burn leaded regular or no-lead premium—a big help, although it doesn't sound that way.

Next came an oil-control package, consisting of added drain lines from the rocker boxes to the sump, and improved valve guides and seals. The alternator's output was increased, the better to keep up with demands from the added lights, radios, heated rider suits and so forth.

Now we get into more confusion. As will be described Harley came out with a new model line in 1971. It was a mixture of FL (big twin) and XL (Sportster) parts. The letter designation was FX, which made sense, and the name was Super Glide. In 1978 one of the FX models was given a toothed-belt final drive, rather than a chain.

It was a mixture of radical and cautious; radical in the sense of trying something new and cautious because Harley didn't try the new things on all the models at once.

The FLT was the now-familiar 80 cu. in. Shovelhead engine in a new and different frame. Note cone cover, shape of oil tank wrapped around new rear frame section and solidly mounted seat. You can't see vibration-absorbing engine mounts, nor five speeds in gearbox. *Road Rider* photo.

This logic led in 1981 to another new model line, lettered FXR and named Super Glide II (later dropped). It's mentioned here because the new line put the Electra Glide, and to a certain extent the FLT Tour Glide, into partial eclipse. The important engineering work was being done on the newer models.

Thus the 1981 special edition collector model (lower case here) was the Heritage, an FLH-80 with suspended seat, fringed leather saddlebags and a windshield, not the full fairing. Accessories from the past, in other words. Case guards were added and the paint was orange and near-olive-drab, a combination that looks much better than it sounds.

In 1982 the FLT (no numbers for the engine because the 80 was the only engine offered) got lower floorboards, new handlebars, new seat, improved seals and locks for the top box and bags, a new primary chain oiler, higher alternator output and a low-maintenance alternator. The FLH was virtually a carry-over.

As a demonstration of concern for quality, the factory prepared two FLTs, sealed the oil tanks and rode them from Vancouver, British Columbia, to Daytona Beach, Florida. They had no problems.

In 1983 the FLH got the toothed-belt final drive, while the FLT still had the enclosed chain. That's what you get when you mix and match parts: The FLH had four speeds but when five speeds were put in the gearbox for the FLT, it was made wider; the belt was wider than the chain so there wasn't room for both. The FLT's suspension was made stiffer and the seat was given less padding so advertised seat height, a major item for the ad department, could be reduced by 1.5 in.

The new 1983 model was the FLHT. Another case of mixed letters, as it has the FLT frame and five-speed transmission and tri-mount vibration-isolating engine mounts and steering geometry.

But because traditionalists didn't like the look of the new fairing, but did want the five speeds and the reduced vibration, the FLHT has the older-style bar-mount fairing.

The model line had been thinned; there were fewer of the older FLH-type machines and more of the FXR models. The original FL versions were the FLH Electra Glide Belt Drive, the FLT and FLHT Tour Glides and the FLT and FLHT Classics, meaning they came with larger top box and extra dressing.

Late in 1983, in time for the announcement of the 1984 model year, there was another headline: A new engine, the V2 Evolution motor.

In keeping with Harley tradition, it wasn't all new. Rather, it was alloy cylinders and heads, vastly improved, with better everything else, all mounted on the by-now classic 80 in. cases. In short, the V2 was the fourth version, the fourth top end, fourth or fifth set of cases and the third displacement of that first ohv V-twin from 1936.

But that properly belongs in the next chapter. For here, the V2 engine meant the last production run for the Shovelhead came in June 1984. The two engines were both made during that year. The Shovel was in the FLH Electra Glide Classic (four speeds and rigid mounts) and in three versions of the FX Super Glide. At the end of the model year there was a special run. The last true FLH was

No dual tanks for the FLT. Instead, a locking panel for the central filler. The ignition switch was on the top clamp and the instrument panel was also on the bars. *Road Rider* photo.

built as the FLHX, deluxe, and the FLHS, stripped. Both had either white or black paint with gold trim. The factory says there were 1,250 examples of the X, and 500 of the S.

What to look for

We might better call this a survey of shortcomings. There are eighteen years of Shovelheads to look at, and while they are alike (they all have electric start, suspension at both ends and so on), they are different and they have different flaws.

In general, all you'll find on the market will be lots of FLHs and a few FLs. There were police, escort, parade and sidecar models, and a few people may have ordered hand shift and foot clutch but their share of the market was tiny.

Nor need we worry a lot about engine codes and numbers. Until 1970, the engine said what it was, as in FLH or FL. Between 1970 and 1980 there were different codes: FL, 1A; FLH, 2A; FLHS, 7E; FLH-80, 3G; 1979 Classic, 3G; and 1980 Classic, 3H.

From 1980 on there was still another system. (Theft was a problem and still is, and the government encouraged the manufacturers to devise long and complicated ways to identify machines and make it more difficult to alter the numbers.) From 1981, the letters were: FLH-80, AA; FLH Police, AB; FLH Classic, AG; Sidecar, AG; FLH Heritage, AJ; and FLHS-80, AK.

As another general theme, during most of the time we're looking at here, the engines used oil. The first version of the Harley ohv V-twin came when all engines burned and dribbled oil. Nor did anybody expect formulated lubricants in aerosol cans. So Harley installed chain oilers that dribbled onto the final chain, and oilers that were supposed to lubricate the primary chain and then return the oil to the tank. There were several versions of this, none of which worked perfectly; be ready to clean your Shovelhead often.

Based on owner surveys, magazine tests and memories of dealers and factory people, here are some of the changes and quirks:

The 1966 through 1969 models used generators. They and their regulators gave trouble and the output wasn't quite enough to keep the battery charged if the starter was used every few miles and/or the headlight was on all the time.

In 1970 came the alternator and ignition inside the timing case. That mostly cured the battery problem, but alas, the kick starter was deleted, which means the alternator *better* keep the battery up.

Weak brakes were a common complaint until 1972, when the drums were replaced with discs. Most people feel the muscular exertion required by the discs is high but the discs do stop better.

There were serious engine failures—flywheels, crankpins, bearings and the like—1965 through 1973. This is where the anti-AMF talk came from, although it was more likely the result of outmoded production equipment pushed too hard. The good news is that these failures will have occurred already and (one hopes) been cured by newer and better parts.

An owner survey in *Road Rider* in 1975 said comfort was the Electra Glide's best feature; vibration and lack of quality control were the worst, notably for the 1970 through 1974 examples. Owners complained about the messy engine caused by the chain oilers.

In 1977 *Road Rider* readers reported getting an average of 23,000 miles from the gearbox, 24,000 from the generator, 28,000 from the regulator, 42,000 from the alternator and 24,000 from the headlight bulb. The most common failure was with the speedometer; why, I cannot imagine.

Road Rider's 1978 survey repeated most of the above, adding that Electra Glides got 40 mpg and 870 mpqt. of oil. The finicky carburetor was a thing of the past, thanks to Keihin.

The FLH got a longer sprung seat in 1977, which was rated better than the earlier buddy seat but not as good as the sprung police solo saddle, probably the best perch ever put on a Harley (perhaps on any motorcycle).

FLT owners were surveyed by *Road Rider* in 1982. They reported 47 mpg and 700 mpqt. The factory replied to this survey that the new oil system, new rings and seals, and a breather routed to the airbox would improve that last figure to 1,400 mpqt., which it seems to have done.

There were still valve and electrical problems, for which there are cures. The valve problem was worst in 1978 through 1980. Fuel quality was poor, the valve guides and top end were weak and the compression ratio was too high. These parts can be replaced with 1981 lower-compression pistons, guides and gaskets, and the engine will run much better.

The weak electrical link was the plug for the connection between the alternator inside the primary case and the regulator on the frame. The plug worked loose; not enough to fall out where its failure could be seen, but just enough to break the electrical connection so the battery didn't get charged. The lights dimmed and finally the engine stopped. (I and an FX with this problem were once towed three miles by a Honda 350. Poor little thing.)

The factory has revised this plug four times. It may still come loose. Silicone seal and constant vigilance are the answer here.

Early examples of Harley electronic ignitions, the Prestolite and later V-Fire systems, had scattered failures. They work pretty well now, but those who don't trust black boxes and irreparable parts may wish to remove same and replace them with the mechanical breaker points and advance weights used on alternator Shovels from 1970 through early 1978. The drive system, outboard of the camshaft under the cone, is the same for all post-timer big twins, so it's no major project.

Oil was under control by 1982 and the V2 engine was cleaner than Caesar's wife, but that's another story.

The Harley-Davidson FLH Electra Glide is the epitome of big motorcycles.

When I use the word epitome I use it correctly. The FLH isn't the perfect machine. Rather, it's the perfect example, the golden average, the blueprint of what a big bike should be. Check the competition, the touring machines from Honda, Yamaha, Suzuki and Kawasaki. They look as much like an FLH as they can get away with.

The FLH is different. It can't be understood nor truly valued in less than a week on the road, at which time even the cynic realizes the gait is matched to the rider's relaxed mind. The ride is a rocking chair, the posture majestic.

And they don't make them any more.

Fearless prediction: The FLH is going to appreciate.

Odd, in a way. For years Harley has made the point that its machines don't lose their value at nearly the rate other motorcycles do. And they didn't, but in large measure this was because the new ones were a lot like the old ones, so there wasn't pressure to trade for a new one.

This has changed. By any measure the V2 engine is better than the Shovelhead. The FLT is a better way to take two people on long trips on two wheels than the FLH. The FXRs and FXRT are better engineered than either the FLH or the FLT.

Now there's reason to trade for a new Harley and people are doing it, bringing down the price of a used one.

Meanwhile, other people are beginning to realize just how good the FLH looks and sounds. They haven't articulated this yet, nor will they until everybody has read this book. (Don't lend this to your friends. Make them

FLT's final-drive chain was enclosed (this one has been cut away for display purposes). The chain got its own lubricant, so the primary case could be closed and the chain oiler discarded. The chain lasts longer and needs less frequent adjustment. *Road Rider* photo.

buy their own copies, after you have scooped up the bargains.)

My guess here is that a good FLH, in particular a good older example perhaps not carrying all the extras, will draw admiring glances while the Wings, Ventures and Vulcans fade into the background.

Year and model	1980 FLT-80 (Tour Glide)
Engine	ohv 45° V-twin
Bore and stroke	3.50x4.25 in.
Displacement	82 cu. in.
BHP	65 (est.)
Gearbox	5 speeds
Shift	left foot
Wheelbase	62.5 in.
Wheels	16 in.
Suspension	telescopic forks, swing-arm rear
Weight	781 lb., tank half full
Seat height	29.5 in.
MPG	42
Top speed	91 mph

Rating: Five becomes three

For evaluation, we can divide the Shovelhead Electra Glide (and the Tour Glide) into groups.

1966 through 1969

Five stars. These are the ones with kick start and outside ignition. Most will have small saddlebags (useful because there's no toolbox) and perhaps a windshield. Don't subtract if a good one has the full bar-mount fairing; don't pay extra for it, either.

FLH owners tend to take care of their bikes. No abuse, but seldom perfection. You can expect the early troubles to have been cured; that is, if the crankpin was going to break it would have broken years ago. Expect to replace the generator and regulator. Or install a solid state regulator and if you get fed up, check the accessory stores and switch to a VW generator. (Yes, it adapts.) Use chain lube and shut off the chain oiler, degrease the ooze from the primary case, tighten the exhaust bolts regularly and if you ride in a manner that makes you stop in a hurry, go for the later disc front brake. If the carburetor acts up once too often, Mikunis work fine and you get a complete kit from the importer.

1970 through 1980

Four stars. First, you may need to repair the weaknesses that came with the bike, as in the valvetrain. You may need to hunt up a sprung saddle, unless you like the solid mount. These models all have the alternator, though, and if they don't have the front disc brake one will bolt right on.

Don't pay extra for the 1973 or 1976 anniversary models. Well, do it if you want to, but other people aren't, at least I haven't found anybody who did, or would.

The same applies to the 80 engine. It's more like a final selling pitch than a genuine better thing to have. The extra power is there, sure, but none of these models are going to win races. Get the 80 if you can; don't pay for it if you don't have to.

Three stars for the FLT. Sorry to harp on this, but although the FLT is better in daily—okay, Sunday or vacation—use it doesn't have the tradition. An FLT is a used motorcycle and an FLT with a V2 engine is better than one with a Shovelhead engine. Thus, the early FLT is a used motorcycle and likely to remain so.

1981 through 1984

Three stars. First, exceptions: The 1982 Heritage model was a modern package trimmed in the old style. Lovely machine, the sort that inspires people to congratulate you on the restoration when all you've done is wash off the grunge and polish the paint and chrome. Even so, I'd only pay a bit extra for this one.

Much the same applies to the last of the genuine FLHs, the X and S models made at the end of the Shovelhead's production run. They probably were bought by people who knew they were the last of their kind and will be priced accordingly. *Maybe* you, the second owner, can charge the third owner more than you paid the first owner. But probably not.

The regular examples of this time, the FLH and FLT, are between the classic era and the more modern V2 engine. They are good solid machines. If you want extra passenger room and luggage capacity, the FLH and FLT with top box have more of both than does the FXRT. The Shovelhead FLH and FLT are solid three-star bikes, worth buying and maintaining, but neither is really an investment.

V2 Evolution Engines: FLT and FLHT

1984-92

Evolution is Harley-Davidson's official name for the current big twin, along with the designation V2; presumably that's shorthand for V-twin, new generation.

The V2 is evolution. It's also a display case, to show the public what Harley engineers can do with the resources available. For the bottom line, though, the V2 is simply a better engine than the ones that came before it.

Diligent readers will recall that Harley-Davidson was a privately held corporation, then an undercapitalized public corporation, then a subsidiary of a larger conglomerate. The parent (AMF) invested in the facilities and kept H-D going but put more money into the plant than the product. When H-D executives bought back the company, they moved as quickly as possible to correct and improve the product and to expand the product line. We've seen the FLT Tour Glide, the tri-mount (rubber) mounts between drivetrain and frame, and we've referred to new models introduced under the Super Glide label.

The V2 engine was a major part of this improvement program. The cylinders were alloy with iron liners, while the cylinders of earlier engines were cast iron. The V2 had new heads. Emissions rules and poor gas have forced all motoring engineers to learn more about combustion chambers. The V2 had its valves set at a narrower included angle, which gave a straighter path for incoming and outgoing gases and allowed a flatter combustion chamber shaped to control the flame front, for higher compression ratio with less octane demand. Further, the V2's electronic ignition had two advance curves, which varied ignition advance as conditions warranted. Camshaft timing, duration and lift were dictated by computer. All this and myriad other details added up to an engine that was stronger, lighter and cleaner. It burned regular, no-lead gas with a higher compression ratio. It developed more power and torque and used less gas and oil. The V2 is as good an engine as there is on the market, never mind that the basic design appeared in 1936.

What can one expect? *Cycle World* introduced the V2 engine in a test of the 1984 FLHTC in its November 1983 issue. The FLHT meant the new frame, five speeds, isolating engine mounts and the different front end of the Tour Glide, but with the bar-mount fairing first seen on the FLH Electra Glide. The C stood for the larger top box and some extra trim. (Harley still used the Electra Glide name for the FLHT, but I think that's a bit misleading.)

Harley incorporates improvements as they prove themselves, so the 1984 FLT and FLHT got air-adjusted rear shocks and anti-dive forks first seen on the 1983 FXRS.

Cycle World was impressed by the V2 FLHTC. It had a 63 in. wheelbase, a test weight (taken with half a tank of gas) of 762

The Evolution engine was just an engine, that is, it attached to the primary case and thus to the separate gearbox. The aluminum cylinders, cylinder heads and rocker boxes were new and the cases were different in detail from that first ohv V-twin but the ancestry can be seen clearly. The camshaft lived below the center of the vee, working pushrods inside the tubes, and the electronic ignition's trigger was under the polished cone cover for the timing case. The oil pump was on the back of the timing case, at the engine's rear and the viewer's left. The V2 engine was better in every way, and had an almost unblemished service record.

lb. It came stock with tubeless Dunlop Touring Elite tires on cast wheels. Final drive was by enclosed chain.

Top speed after a half-mile run was 96 mph, 0-60 took 6.9 sec. and the standing quarter mile came up in 14.9 sec. with a trap speed of 86.2 mph. A ride around a controlled loop returned 47 mpg, with 50 mpg and up available at steady and prudent highway speeds.

Oil consumption was too low to be measured. Everything worked and nothing broke. The test riders liked the gearbox, the engine, the brakes and the various controls, except perhaps Harley's turn signal switches, which required thumb pressure rather than being flipped on and flipped off (or forgotten, which is why Harley made you hold them on). I should say here, so I don't forget, that if you don't like the factory buttons, the factory offered an accessory kit that lets you flip on/off—but if you forget, don't blame them or me. The only serious shortcoming noted was a choppy ride on the freeway, which no amount of juggling air pressure got rid of.

In mid-year 1984 there was another major improvement. From their inception until this change, the big twins used a dry clutch. Most motorcycles used clutch plates that ran in an oil bath. Harleys have always had trouble keeping the primary chain lubricated. One of the problems here is that it shared housing space with the clutch, and the clutch wasn't supposed to be oiled.

As a possible cure, a belt primary drive was offered by accessory firms and for a time by the factory. But although the belt final

Engine aside, the V2 Tour Glide looked just about identical to the Shovelhead Tour Glide. *Road Rider* photo.

drive worked better than anybody dared hope, the enclosed environment of the primary belt was hostile and the belts didn't last as long as they should have; the factory went back to using a primary chain.

The final solution was a new clutch spring, a diaphragm spring, which looked sort of like a flower except the (metal) petals radiated inward. It was one piece, a disc, while conventional clutches used a set of oil springs. And the diaphragm spring could exert more pressure on the clutch plates while needing less pressure from the rider's hand. Further, because rider effort was less while clutch pressure was higher, the clutch plates could run in oil, keeping them cool, providing lubricant for the primary chain and letting the primary case be enclosed so there weren't leaks and seeps.

Sounds too good to be true, eh? It works better than it sounds. It's wonderful. The lighter clutch lever means you needn't plan or dread shifting. You can slip the clutch

Giant top box and saddlebags will hold all your gear for weeks on the road. The Tour Glide came with a set of tools, something Harley left out for nearly 20 years. *Road Rider* photo.

The 1985 (and 1984) FLHT Electra Glide had a lower operator seat, a higher passenger seat and a bar-mount fairing. Otherwise, it was just like the FLT Tour Glide. Harley-Davidson photo.

and find neutral the first time. A great improvement.

For the 1985 FL-series V2 models, the engineers managed to find space for the final-drive belt and the five-speed gearbox, so all the 1985s had belts as well as the new clutch, some minor graphic changes, yet another change to the locks on the luggage and some wiring revisions (the starter didn't always disengage cleanly in 1984).

The 1986 FL line was mostly as it had been, save for some changes like round (and less intrusive) air cleaners. There was a Liberty—as in Statute of—Edition of the FLHT and all Harleys that model year got front turn signal lights that stayed on with the headlight, the better to be seen.

For 1987, in what sounds like a contradiction in terms, the FLH line got the FLHS, for Sport. Lightest and most nimble of the full tourers, Sport in this case meant a windshield instead of a fairing. It also meant the lowest sticker price in the FL line, which didn't hurt.

Making the news even briefer, there were no new models for 1988. Well, there was one late-breaking FLS, but that doesn't concern us here.

The FL line was topped in 1989 by two added models, the FLTC Tour Glide Ultra Classic and FLHTC Electra Glide Ultra Classic. As you'd infer, the T used the frame-mount fairing and the H had the old bar-mount fairing. The Ultras, if one can shorten

The 1986 FLTC (and the other FLs as well) could easily be identified by its round air cleaners and 2-into-1 exhaust. Seatbacks and fairing interiors and instrument panels were revised for the model year but the basic package—V2 engine, five speeds, belt drive and full touring equipment—remained. These are big, specialized motorcycles. Because they represent such a large investment and such a controlled rate of gradual change, they're not likely to depreciate much in the foreseeable future. Harley-Davidson photo.

all those letters and names, had the normal full complement of boxes and bags and lights, plus cruise control, CB radio, the most complete sound system one can imagine, fairing lowers with stowage and special paint. Pause for breath.

The five FLs carried over into the 1990 model year with normal mods, as in a new clutch for all the 80s and details improvements—it's fun to read this year what was wrong with last year—to the cruise controls and intercoms on the Ultras. The same applies for 1991, in which shortcomings of the intercom and footpegs were the big news.

Strike that. The real news for 1991 has to be the return of the sidecar, with two models for the FLs. Charming as always, if a bit difficult to imagine as an actual mode of transportation.

And in 1992, more detail changes and subtle modifications.

The obvious conclusion here is that the FL series, in each and all of the five versions, had pretty much gone as far as it can go. That isn't a complaint, because the FL has surely come a long way. And it makes the job of choosing and evaluating fairly simple.

What to look for

First, a different set of cautions: These are nearly new models, so there need be no concern with getting a 61 when you thought it was a 74, or buying two case sides that don't fit together.

Let it be stated here that the FLT and FLHT are large motorcycles. They're heavy. The seats may be low but they're also wide; ditto for the frame sides and the floorboards. Fully dressed and loaded touring bikes demand rider skill, especially at low speeds, not because they're poorly designed but because

The FLHS Electra Glide Sport came with luggage bags and rack but no top box, and with a windshield instead of a full fairing. It was the cheapest of the FL line. Harley-Davidson photo.

they are so big, heavy and wide when you need to put your foot down in a hurry.

In short, an FLT or FLHT is not a first motorcycle. What they offer is a relaxed gait, armchair comfort and the ability to travel on any major highway at highway speeds while burdened with lots of people and luggage. The bags and box on the FLT and FLHT are larger than those used on the FXRT. The seat, especially for the passenger, is bigger and softer and comes with something to lean on, welcome after hours on the road. I'm not downgrading these models, merely letting you know the pros and cons.

In terms of equipment, for myself I wouldn't get the early 1984 if I could find a late 1984, the one with the diaphragm clutch spring, at the same price or even higher.

The FL (big twin) V2 models were made during the three model years 1984 through 1986. They came in two versions, the plain Tour Glide with full fairing and the Electra Glide FLHT with the old bar-mount fairing, and in regular or Classic trim, with the larger top box. (One might add the FLT/TLE sidecar and the police versions of the T and the HT, except they're all rare and unlikely to be on the market for a few years.)

The V2 engine has had some random failures; for instance, the sticking starter. The plug between the alternator and regulator still comes loose. And if a V2 is parked on its side stand for a few weeks, oil will seep down from the tank to the sump and when the engine is started the surplus oil will bloop up into and then out of the air box, never mind

The FLTC Tour Glide Ultra Classic was, as the name hints, more of everything you could put on a motorcycle, down to CB radio, floorboards for the passenger and windbreakers for the riders' legs. Harley-Davidson photo.

that the factory says there are drains from the box to take care of that.

The starter must have continued to give trouble because in 1986 the factory increased cranking power by eliminating the relay. All the FLs got a lighter and quieter rear brake, another hint of a problem not directly discussed, and all Harleys got new intake and exhaust systems to meet new federal noise limits.

Changes aimed at the customer included floorboards for the passenger, adjustable boards for the operator and a new seatback/ grab rail. The letter C, as in FLHTC and FLTC, represented a 40-watt stereo sound system as standard, while paint and trim were the same for all models.

In terms of equipment, what we have is a straight sort of lapsed time frame; in general, each model is a couple of notches better than the one that preceded it. The V2 engine beats the Shovelhead, belt drive is nicer than chain, the diaphragm clutch works more easily than the coil spring version. This extends down to the more recent 80s having an alternator plug that can't work loose and there's a new oil pump that won't sump and controls to keep the oil from getting into the sump when the bike sits for a few weeks.

Rating: Three more stars

One reason Harleys didn't used to depreciate at the average rate has been that they didn't change much. As we've seen, that's no longer so, and that means they lose value or get cheaper just like the other scoots.

The gain here is that the newer ones really are better than the older models, especially the FL series. A 1990 FLT has more goodies and a better drivetrain than a 1980 FLT, simple as that.

A big new Harley costs a lot of money. It's a purchase that isn't taken lightly. Nor do Harley buyers trade for the New! New! New! machine every model year. Thus, there aren't many used V2-powered bikes on the market. They'll sell for less than the new ones, and the older they are the less they'll sell for because they aren't as improved. All in scale, all logical, just as the one you buy new will be less valuable next year. Not much less, but some.

And one more time, this isn't to say a used FLT or FLHT isn't a good buy.

Year and model	1986 FLTC (Tour Glide)
Engine	ohv 45° V-twin
Bore and stroke	3.50x4.25 in.
Displacement	82 cu. in.
BHP	55 (est. net)
Gearbox	5 speeds
Shift	left foot
Wheelbase	62.9 in.
Wheels	16 in.
Suspension	telescopic forks, swing-arm rear
Weight	787.5 lb. (curb)
Seat height	31.3 in.
MPG	45
Top speed	90 mph (est.)

Chapter 2

★★★★★	FX 1971, Sturgis 1991
★★★★	Low Rider 1978, Sturgis 1980
★★★★	Softail
★★★	All others

Super Glides

During the turmoil of the late sixties—when Harley-Davidson was being acquired by American Machine and Foundry, when increased demand led to decreased quality, when the workers were unhappy and the customers confused—somebody at Harley nonetheless managed to know what was going on out there in the real world.

The result was the Super Glide, an uncannily accurate expression of what lots of people wanted in a motorcycle. It was at the same time a practical combination of components already on hand; two plus two equaled five.

Background: By the late sixties the big Harleys had grown into bigger Harleys, fully equipped for trips on the road but a bit clumsy in daily use. The FL and FLH Electra Glides were rewarding motorcycles, but not exciting ones.

The Sportster, meanwhile, alternated between acting as a junior FLH and a performance machine, handicapped by the arrival from England and Japan of rivals with more power and cylinders.

While that was going on for new bikes, owners of used big twins were inventing the chopper.

People are funny. When bikes (or cars) come stripped, enthusiasts put things on them. When the factories added the extras, enthusiasts began taking things off. So there arose the customized un-dresser, you could say, with skimpy seat, no case guards or extra lights, no front fender and a rear fender that was cut back or replaced with the one from the front. The beginning was probably the semi-racer, known then as a bob-job, but the name chopper (as in everything surplus to actually running down the road was chopped off) became the generic term. Choppers acquired high handlebars and, because they forced the riders to lean back in the saddle, extra foot pegs were mounted on the frame in front of the engine; highway pegs, they're now called.

This enthusiasm didn't go unnoticed. Willie G. Davidson, grandson of one of the company's founders, a designer by training and a motorcycle nut by both birth and choice, was (and still is) head of H-D design and styling. He's too modest and smart to take credit here, but the Super Glide almost surely came from or through him.

The first FX

For model year 1971, that is, late in calendar year 1970, Harley introduced the Super Glide. Its letters were FX, F from the FLH and X from the XL and XLH. Made sense: The FX used the frame, rear suspension and 74 Shovelhead engine from the FL line, with the XL Sportster's forks and 19 in. front wheel. The engine was a cone engine, an Alternator Shovelhead, but the electric starter was removed.

At the time, Harley-Davidson had branched out into golf carts and other things, and had a fiberglass plant. The first Super Glide (and an earlier optional Sportster) took

The first FX Super Glide was a mix—FLH frame and Alternator Shovelhead 74 engine, twin tanks with console from the FLH, but with Sportster forks and headlight, and a one-piece fiberglass rear fender and seat base. *Road Rider* photo.

For its second year, the Super Glide lost the fiberglass panels and got a conventional rear fender and scalloped dual seat—stylish if hard on the occupants. Harley-Davidson photo.

advantage of this and used a fiberglass rear fender and seat base, above which went a stylish if skimpy seat cushion. The fuel tank was a dual unit, as on the FLH.

This machine was a radical departure, albeit several other makes, notably Norton, did similar things with fiberglass in that period. To set off the difference, the Super Glide could be ordered with a red, white and blue paint scheme.

Considering that the tour-oriented magazine would have preferred the cushy sprung seat and floorboards of the FLH, *Road Rider* gave the new model high marks. The FX was lighter and quicker, stopped shorter than the FLH did, and was stable at 120 (indicated or timed, not known).

Because the FX shared the 74 engine, it also had that engine's problems, such as a Teflon-coated ignition cam that wore early and a Bendix carb (remember the trouble-free label?) that flooded. And testers and owners had trouble starting the beast until they learned the drill: Turn on the fuel petcock, rock the bike back and forth to get gas moving in the bowl, kick through with choke on, ignition and throttle off; then try it with throttle off but ignition on. It worked, usually.

The fiberglass bodywork didn't work in the showroom. For 1972 the FX followed the Sportster into a return to conventional rear fender and separate seat. The ad pitch changed as well. In 1971 the FX was billed as a style mate to the XLCH, while the 1972 ads proclaimed the FX and FLH as "The Road Kings."

Cycle World called the 1972 FX "a Sportster for people who like 74s," which was probably right. *Cycle World*'s starting drill

With its conventional rear fender, stepped seat and single 3.5 gal. tank, the 1974 FXE Super Glide was at the same time more sporting and more normal than the original FX. The FXE didn't have the luggage capacity of the FLH, but it did come with electric start and there wasn't anything on the bike styled to interfere with daily riding. Clean machines, albeit lacking the flamboyance of some later models. Harley-Davidson photo.

was three kicks with ignition live, full choke no throttle when cold; one kick with throttle open when hot. The testers reported the gearbox clunked, the forks were too soft and the brakes weak but the FX returned 47 mpg, topped out at 108 mph, hit 60 mph in 5.6 sec. and covered the standing quarter mile in 14.43 sec. at 92 mph. With the 3.5 gal. tanks half full the FX weighed 559 lb., so it was between the Sportster and the Electra Glide.

The 1973 FX had improved—firmer—suspension, disc brakes and a single 3.5 gal. fuel tank styled after the one the Italians did for the Aermacchi Sprint.

Repeat, people are funny. In 1974 the factory introduced the FXE, E for electric start. This was an option and the FX was still the standard. But just because the Super Glide was marketed as the sports bike for those who didn't need sissy stuff like electric legs, there were buyers who liked the name but didn't wish to work at the game. The FXE was a good move. In 1973 FX sales totaled 7,625. In 1974 the count was 3,034 for the FX and 6,199 for the FXE—a net gain in sales for factory and dealerships.

The FX, sometimes called the FX-1200, and the FXE were mostly unchanged through 1975 and 1976. There was a Liberty Edition FXE in 1976, celebrating the Bi-centennial with black metalflake paint and red, white and blue decorations, and there were various paint options during this period but few mechanical changes showed up in the catalog. Exhaust systems varied. The first FX used two low pipes feeding one muffler on the right; then there were parallel pipes with two mufflers; then siamese headers joined at the cylinders' vee and curving back to one muffler; then two pipes into staggered mufflers, one behind the other, but with a balance tube just below the air cleaner. And there have been hundreds of accessory systems offered during the years. Best tip for restoration here is to search out ads or sales brochures for the model in question.

Super Glides began the 1977 year with revisions to component packaging that let the kick lever (if fitted) tuck closer to the engine and away from the rider's leg. Also, more engine power was claimed although the fac-

The Low Rider was a Super Glide with special paint and trim, low bars and the suspension shortened to bring the seat closer to earth, hence the name. Harley-Davidson photo.

tory didn't say where it came from. One option was a cast rear wheel.

The Low Rider

During the 1977 calendar year a surprise sprang up from which the motorcycle world may not yet have recovered: The model was named the Low Rider, lettered FXS and labeled a 1978 production.

The Low Rider was an FXE except the forks and shocks were shortened and the seat scooped, so static seat height was 27.4 in. from the ground. The forks were extended; that is, they had more of an angle from the vertical and the front wheel was moved away from the frame, making the wheelbase longer. The FXS had cast wheels, triple disc brakes and twin fuel tanks with instruments on the console between them. The handlebars were flat and narrow (drag bars in the vernacular), on risers; short stands bolted to the top clamp. Silver paint was the only choice, while the cases, barrels and heads were finished in black crackle and the fins on heads and barrels were polished.

Cycle World found the ride rough and the handling most unsporting, despite being stable at speed. The test bike got 47 mpg, a 15 sec. quarter mile and a top speed of 98 mph. Weight with half-filled tanks was 623 lb., so electric start and cast wheels added something besides convenience.

The major magazines were mostly puzzled by the Low Rider. Until it arrived everybody had been going in the direction of touring or sport, as in road racing. The Low Rider went another way, appealed to an element respectable people don't like to talk about.

Pause for derisive snort. There were a lot of respectable people who liked the look of latent menace, the crouched, muscular profile of the Low Rider. The FX line was the best selling of Harley's three groups in 1978 and the FXS accounted for nearly half of FX sales.

Success bred expansion. The Low Rider was offered with either black, white or silver paint in 1979, while all the FX models got the electronic ignition and other mechanical changes common to all the Shovelheads that year.

For 1979 there was also the regular Super Glide, still with kick lever although electric start was standard. The Low Rider got what's known as a sissy bar, a short padded frame-

Year and model	1972 FX (Super Glide)
Engine	ohv 45° V-twin
Bore and stroke	3.43x3.96 in.
Displacement	74 cu. in.
BHP	65 (claimed)
Gearbox	4 speeds
Shift	left foot
Wheelbase	62.3 in.
Wheels	19F/16R
Suspension	telescopic forks, swing-arm rear
Weight	559 lb., tank half full
Seat height	29.7 in.
MPG	47 (at 70 mph)
Top speed	108 mph

Year and model	1978 FXS (Low Rider)
Engine	ohv 45° V-twin
Bore and stroke	3.43x3.96 in.
Displacement	74 cu. in.
BHP	65 (est.)
Gearbox	4 speeds
Shift	left foot
Wheelbase	63.5 in.
Wheels	19F/16R
Suspension	telescopic forks, swing-arm rear
Weight	623 lb., tank half full
Seat height	27.4 in.
MPG	47
Top speed	98 mph

Fat Bob was an FXE that returned to the dual fuel tanks of the first FX, plus buckhorn bars. *Road Rider* photo.

work behind the passenger seat so she (usually, don't mean to be sexist) has something to lean on or cling to, and a leather pouch, useful for tools but openly referred to as a stash pouch (wink, nudge).

The Fat Bob

There was also a new model, the Super Glide Fat Bob. The name comes from way back. Stripping a big twin used to include fitting a smaller fuel tank, from an XLCH or even a scooter. I wasn't around then but I'm told if the builder removed all the extras, chopped this and that, but kept the dual tanks, he'd built a Fat Bob—fat for the tanks, bob as in bobbed fenders.

The Super Glide Fat Bob was a Low Rider plus it came with choice of cast or spoke wheels, twin fuel tanks and high—buckhorn in the vernacular—handlebars.

During the 1979 model year the 80 in. version of the Shovelhead engine became an option for the Low Rider and Super Glide.

The Wide Glide

Skipping ahead for a moment, one of the 1980 models was the Wide Glide, lettered FXWG. This was a Fat Bob (FXEF, the F stands for fat) with wider triple clamps, wider front axle, extended forks and a 21 in. front wheel. The Wide Glide had the 80 engine, 5 gal. dual tanks, a bobbed rear fender, buckhorn bars on risers, a small (Sportster) headlight, staggered shorty dual exhausts and brake and shift pedals designed

The Wide Glide was a factory chopper, as contrasted with what later became known as factory customs. The Wide Glide's fork stanchion tubes were farther apart than on other FXs, the rear fender replicated the look of front fenders mounted in back, ditto the stepped seat with sissy bar and backrest, the stash pouch, extended forks, 21 in. front wheel and high bars. Flamed, dual 5 gal. tanks were standard and the foot controls and pegs were mounted well forward (highway pegs, in the vernacular, because that's where you put your feet to lean back in the wind of the open road). Not the most comfortable motorcycle ever made, but that didn't keep the model from selling well. Harley-Davidson photo.

to be operated from the forward-mount (highway) pegs.

The Wide Glide took the concept another giant step. It, the Low Rider and the Fat Bob were basically Super Glides with custom equipment. They went as far toward being choppers as a factory could go, and they sold well.

If they baffled the magazines, they didn't baffle the Japanese factories, whose honest intention was to supply the customer with whatever he or she wanted. Before you could say *Easy Rider* the Big Four had models with stepped seats, high bars, small tanks. Harley once ran an ad, in English and Japanese, with a picture of a Low Rider. "Here," the headline said, "is your next year's model." The next year, Honda came out with a model that looked exactly like the Low Rider. It sold in record numbers.

Some joke.

The Sturgis

Back to the story. The big 1980 technical news came early that spring, with the unveiling of the Sturgis, named after the famous rally in South Dakota.

The Sturgis, lettered FXB, had primary and final drive via toothed belts, developed through the cooperative efforts of Harley and Gates Rubber Company.

Replacing the primary and final chains with belts was more than a bolt-on. Belts are wider than chains of equal strength so the gearbox had to be modified and the starter moved. Next, because the clutch was out-

Engineering improvements aren't always appreciated on the showroom floor, so along with its drive belts the FXB Sturgis got black chrome and paint where the otherwise-identical Low Rider had regular chrome and silver paint. The Sturgis had foot pegs and controls in the usual places, plus highway pegs mounted in front of the engine cases, for an optional place to rest your feet and stretch your legs. The belt final drive has proven to be even better than the factory dared hope, and it is now standard equipment on most big Harleys. The primary belt wasn't as successful and is no longer fitted to new bikes. Harley-Davidson photo.

board of the primary belt and the primary belt was outboard of the final belt, changing that final belt was a chore. No more could one pop off the master link and thread in a new chain by the side of the road. In fact, to reassure a skeptical public, the factory supplied a spare belt that could be clipped on for the ride into the nearest town, kind of like the midget spare tires that come with cars today.

Other than the different drive system—can't say new because all motorcycles used belts, leather ones, at the turn of the century—the Sturgis was a Low Rider, with the 80 engine, new electronic ignition and compression ratio of 8:1 (which proved to be too high).

A side benefit from the belts, though, was a closed breather from crankcase to air cleaner, allowed because the primary belt didn't need lubricant. Nor did the final belt, so there went the chain oiler. Belt-driven bikes stay much cleaner.

Cycle World's scales showed the Sturgis weighed 610 lb. with the 3.5 gal. tanks half full. Testers clocked it at 106 mph for the flying half mile, 14.62 sec. for the standing quarter mile, and 48 mpg for the measured loop. The engine pinged on premium fuel. Because the Sturgis was lighter than the FLT with the same engine, it was geared taller. Passengers didn't like their portion of the seat and a 150 lb. rider (me, as it happened) couldn't start the engine cold with the kick lever.

Road Rider said the front of the seat was good for eight hours, the brakes squealed, but everything else worked fine. Its test bike got 49 mpg on premium.

The factory's first projection was a drive-belt life of 20,000 miles. Because replacement was such a hassle, *Road Rider* suggested the belt be replaced at 14,000 miles, the expected life of the rear tire. Removing and replacing tubeless tires is almost as much work as replacing the belt, so the owner's way out was to take the bike to the dealership and let the shop do both at the same time.

The Sturgis' primary belt was on the inside of the coil-spring clutch and the final belt was inside the primary belt, so replacement takes a few hours. *Road Rider* photo.

Belts aside, the Sturgis was a Fat Bob. Witness the dual tanks and the instruments on the console between them. *Road Rider* photo.

All the magazines found the Sturgis' belts to be an improvement: smoother, quieter and altogether a good thing. Belts were an experiment, as much in customer acceptance as engineering practice, so only 1,500 FXBs were scheduled that first year; factory records show 1,470 were built.

In use, though, the belts worked better than expected. Actual life turned out to be 30,000 or 40,000 miles, plus never having to oil them and seldom having to adjust them

Year and model	1980 FXB-80 (Sturgis)
Engine	ohv 45° V-twin
Bore and stroke	3.50x4.25 in.
Displacement	82 cu. in.
BHP	65 (est.)
Gearbox	4 speeds
Shift	left foot
Wheelbase	64.7 in.
Wheels	19F/16R
Suspension	telescopic forks, swing-arm rear
Weight	610 lb., tank half full
Seat height	27 in.
MPG	48
Top speed	106 mph

The Softail, here in 1985 trim with V2 engine, looked as if it was the rigid rear as seen on the legendary Knucklehead and Panhead models. Harley-Davidson photo.

made the rider's life easier. Buyers accepted the idea and more and more Harleys came with belt final drive. Countering that, of course, was the replacement of the belt primary with the diaphragm spring clutch and sealed primary case.

The new FX

In 1981 the 74 Shovelhead was phased out and the compression ratio of the 80 engine was reduced to 7.4:1 so it would run without knock on regular fuel, leaded or not. Other than that, the Super Glides were carryovers.

There was the twin-belt FXB Sturgis, the FXWG Wide Glide with fuel tanks painted with flames or pinstriped metallic, the FXEF Fat Bob with twin tanks and cast wheels, the FXS Low Rider, or the FXE Super Glide with wire wheels and single tank.

Now we come to a parting of the models.

Late in 1981 Harley unveiled its future, in the form of the FXR and FXRS. Note the initials. These bikes were at first called Super Glide II, implying that they were new versions of the original Super Glide. But they weren't, not really. They were an extension, a result of the work done when planning the FLT, which itself was briefly billed as the Electra Glide II.

The FX and FXR lines were more different than their letters suggest. The FXRs had five-speed gearbox and insulated drivetrain mounts, while the original FX-style machines had four speeds and solid mounts. In 1982 the FX models were FXS Low Rider, FXWG Wide Glide, FXE Super Glide and FXB Sturgis.

Belt drive had been proven in the field by 1983 and there was a merger. The Low Rider became the FXSB and got twin belts, extended forks and some trim changes, while there was no more separate Sturgis in model or name. The Wide Glide came with striped tank on special orders only; the FXE Super Glide was the standard model.

Literally tucked away, below the gearbox and within the frame rails, were the shock/springs for the rear suspension. *Road Rider* photo.

The Softail

Some time back I said something about the Wide Glide going as far as a factory chopper could. Wrong. In 1984 Harley proved the rule by going further. The new model was the FXST Softail. Mostly it was a Wide Glide except for its V2 engine, and the rear section of the frame was much revised.

The idea wasn't new. Several Italian makers used to put the rear spring or springs beneath the engine. In fact, one of Harley's own two-strokes used the idea years ago.

But that was done for space utilization. With the Softail, Harley wanted to recapture the look of the old solid rear suspension (that is, no suspension) of the big twins. An independent engineer designed a triangulated swing arm that looked like the old rigid rear section. He put the pivot up high, hidden by the seat, and the springs and shocks under the gearbox, also out of sight. Harley officials saw the bike at a show, liked it and began to produce it under a royalty agreement.

This rear suspension didn't offer a lot of wheel travel, but then, neither did conventional Harleys. This aside, the Softail was a Wide Glide, with 21 in. front wheel, a single front disc brake and a kick lever. There wasn't room for both five speeds and kick, so because the factory figured the market for the ST was emotional, Harley supplied the kick.

Softail and Wide Glide used a clamshell rider seat and a small pad for the passenger, which most magazines at least didn't like. The foot controls were mounted forward along with the pegs, which could also be awkward (raising one's leg to reach the brake could take valuable time).

The Softail was longer (66.3 in. wheelbase), lower (25 or 26 in., depending on who's measuring) and, of course, wider than anything else on the market. Claimed dry weight was 618 lb., which sounds about right in line with measured weights for the other FX models. The press remarked on the dual fuel tanks, which required one to first fill the left tank, then snug down the cap and fill the

The plain (so to speak) Wide Glide had the older frame, as shown by the forward-mount rear shocks, a 21 in. front wheel and a rear fender that looked like the front fenders chopper guys used to put on the rear. This is a 1985, with V2 engine and good ol' kick start just in case. Harley-Davidson photo.

The Low Rider wasn't as distinctive by 1985, with its dual tanks, cast wheels, sissy bar, V2 engine and so forth, like the others in the FX line. Harley-Davidson photo.

The 1985 Fat Bob was really the basic FX, with the plain rear fender, wire wheels, no sissy bar and no kick start. Harley-Davidson photo.

right tank. (Do it in reverse and gas drains from right to left while you pump.)

Road Rider got 47 mpg from a Softail, *Bike* (an English magazine) got 46. Both said the V2 engine used less oil than they could measure. Mark that problem as solved.

Other 1984 news was that the Wide Glide, with Shovelhead engine, rigid mounts and four speeds, got belt final drive with chain primary. The Low Rider kept the same drivetrain and the FXE Super Glide, the basic model, had primary and final chains.

Because the Shovelhead engine went out of production in mid-1984, the 1985 FX (and FXR and FL) models all got the V2 engine.

This brought some other changes. Although the final belt worked better than hoped for, the primary belt didn't. There were some failures in the original Sturgis. Tensioners supposed to keep the belts tight gave out early and the belts rubbed against the case. The hot and humid enclosure wasn't healthy, so the primary belt was replaced with reliable old chain as a running change during 1984.

However, using the V2 engine meant the FX models could also use the new clutch, which ran in oil. So, for 1985 all four solid-mount Glides, FXEF Fat Bob, FXWG Wide Glide, FXSB Low Rider and FXST Softail, got the new clutch; Low Rider and Wide Glide came with final belt drive.

For 1986 the FX line was narrowed. The Fat Bob and Low Rider models were dropped and the Low Rider name was transferred to the FXRS, formerly the Low Glide.

Top of the FX line was the new-for-1986 FXSTC, the Softail Custom. It had the solid rear wheel first seen on the Disc Glide, plus black-painted engine with chromed aluminum covers, red/burgundy paint with burgundy accents on the black frame and a thicker seat with sissy bar. The Custom and the plain Softail now had the five-speed gearbox and belt drive. The Softails have proven very popular so it's likely they'll hold their value in the future. Harley-Davidson photo.

The Softail was joined by a Softail Custom, with extra paint and chrome and a solid rear wheel, as first seen on the Disc Glide, which also is no longer a separate model. The FXST and FXSTC got the five-speed gearbox and belt final drive.

The only classic, so to speak, Super Glide left by 1986 was the FXWG, the only big twin with four speeds and the only Harley with kick start.

The Softail line-up was expanded in 1987 with the FLST Heritage Softail Special. The word here should be Retro, as they say in art circles. The Special had black-and-chrome for the engine and gearbox, with the body colors of blue and cream, as seen in the 1950s. The Special came with windshield, leather saddlebags with studs and conchos (the silver things) and a larger seat with backrest. What it was, was what people did for themselves forty years earlier.

The Motor Company took a huge leap into nostalgia early in 1988. For the company's 85th anniversary, having said there'd be no new models for the year, they introduced the Springer.

We need some background for this: Back when the Davidsons and William Harley got serious about motorcycles, Harley quit his job and went back to school to get the

The Springer, formally lettered FXSTS, began as a stripped Softail fitted with a new, improved version of the leading link, coil sprung, forks used on the very first Harleys. They were more closely controlled and work perfectly well, albeit with less comfort than the telescopic forks provide. Harley-Davidson photo.

Nostalgic suspension and buckhorn bars or no, careful design made the Springer a spirited, if not quite sporting, ride. *Cycle World*

The Fat Boy, as the FLSTF was called, used solid wheels and grey paint for body panels and frame to give a solid, one-piece, heavy-as-it-is look unique in motorcycling. Harley-Davidson photo.

engineering degree he knew he'd need. While doing that, he designed a front suspension, the leading links seen on Harley-Davidsons from then until 1949 and so good other makers copied them under license.

In 1988, H-D brought the leading links, called Springers because of the visible coil springs right out there in front, back.

Obviously, this was marketing. What you do after you make a rear suspension that looks like it isn't a suspension, after you go back to leather from fiberglass, is make the front end look as classic/antique as the rest of the machine.

Less obviously, the engineering department had done extra work and used computers and all the aids Bill Harley didn't have when he sketched up the Springer forks in study hall. The new front, like the Softail rear, works perfectly well. There's no loss of control. Instead, you have less wheel travel and thus less comfort.

This was a trade-off the buyers, who turned up in droves, accepted without qualm. The rest of the FLSTS was normal FLS, as in solid engine mounts, five speeds, spoke wheels and so on. One suspects the radical front got people into the showrooms and Harleys into the magazines, too, and that didn't hurt.

Equally different, if not as Retro, was the 1990 new model, the Fat Boy.

The FLSTF (you can work these out by now, right?) was a Softail mechanically, but fitted with a disc front wheel, fully valanced front fender, widely spaced dual exhausts in what's known as Shotgun style and wide, as in FLH, bars. Paint was silver, with dark yellow highlights, a combo that looks better than it sounds. Again it was a limited edition and again the new model sold well.

Repeating a sort of dual Harley theme, somebody was taking notes and assigning resources, limited of course, to where they'd do the most good.

In the case of the rigid-engine Super Glides, which were all Softails by this time, there was no news during model years 1991 and 1992. Early in calendar year 1992, at their Daytona Beach show, H-D introduced a trim package, called the Heritage Nostalgia. It was billed as a 1993 model because it wouldn't

Leading-link suspension followed the design of the original, but it was stronger, more predictable and more durable on the modern Springer. Note the care with which the brake was located on/by the axle and fork leg. *Cycle*

actually be on sale until August 1992, when the rest of the '93s were introduced.

Odd way to do business and it indicated, to me at least, that nostalgia wasn't as good as it used to be. You can look back only so far for so long and although the Softails have done good business and the various variations sold well, the limit had been reached. You can't take back good brakes or install oil leaks, can you?

What to look for

First warning, as they say along Arizona highways: The Super Glide was designed to meet the demands of a particular market. As a rule, from then until now, the factory emphasized form more than function. The low, stepped seats and the high bars feel fine in town and for short runs. But because they prop the rider up in the wind, and because the rear sections of the seats are usually small, Super Glides become tiring and cramped on the open road. (I know, you see people out there on them. I don't say it can't be done, only that it takes more dedication than most of us have.)

Next, the nature of the market. Electra Glides appeal to the mature buyer, one who will maintain the investment. Sportsters often are neglected, even abused.

Super Glides get modified. Again, a generalization. But the Super Glides appeal to lifestylers, who also like power and noise and looking different. Thus, the average used Super Glide is more likely to have big-bore pistons, stroker flywheels, hot cam, modified exhausts. Brakes may have been added or subtracted, tanks swapped, forks extended.

Look out. Unless you yourself are an experienced mechanic or know somebody in whose skill you have total faith, walk away.

Beyond that are the ordinary cautions. The FX arrived after the advent of the alternator, so you're spared generator problems. The drum brakes ('71 and '72) were weaker than the discs. All Harleys 1971 through 1974 were bothered by poor quality control, although most of the failures from then will have been fixed by now. The Shovelhead engine had too much compression for its own good 1978 through 1980. And they all used oil until perhaps the oil control kit of 1982, surely by the arrival of the V2 engine for the Softail in 1984 and the others in 1985. However, there have been reports of drips from the new primary case and airbox—not as bad as they used to be, though.

The other chronic bother, the plug that came loose and disconnected the alternator, was supposedly taken care of. Further, the general flow of engineering improvements has been so effective that any of the Super Glides, make that any Harley-Davidson, built

Odd for a traditional look, but the Heritage Nostalgia, like the Fat Boy on which it's strongly based, goes against Harley-Davidson habits in that it's called an FL, the FLSTN, while it has the FXST chassis. But they put the fat front wheel and big forks, as in FL, on the ST frame, so that's where the letter came from. Aside from that, the Nostalgia was an early 1993, introduced in March 1992, and had full Retro style plus wide whitewall tires. Harley-Davidson photo.

since 1985 will perform well under normal use. Watch for the errant oil leak and that's all you'll have to worry about.

Rating: On the curve

No sooner had Harley-Davidson invented the factory chopper than it had to keep one step ahead of the clones. And a lot of the changes were in style; that is, the newer FXs made more demands, while being better mechanically, than the first ones. Even so. . . .

Five stars: The original FX Super Glide of 1971

This is guesswork. But Harley only made 4,700 that first year, as buyers weren't too sure about the idea. They looked as different as they were; unique, even. The original version was a milestone and thus is more likely to gain in value.

Price, I don't know. I can't recall ever seeing one for sale. And because some of the body parts and trim were made for just that one year they're going to be more difficult to find if you want a perfect restoration. Against that, the 1971 is reasonably comfortable, no extremes in control or posture, so it could be worth the hunt.

Four stars: 1978 Low Rider and 1980 Sturgis

The same reasoning applies here. The first Low Rider was the spark for a host of imitations, none of which quite captured the true spirit. The first Sturgis had that style and it also had the new and valuable belt drive. Neither is quite as different as the first Super Glide was and they're newer, so there's less effort in keeping one up or returning it to as-new condition. (Okay, because the Sturgis was a limited run, one may be hard to find.) Neither the Low Rider nor the Sturgis had as strong an engine as the first FX did, but that can be fixed.

Year and model	1985 FXST (Softail)
Engine	ohv 45° V-twin
Bore and stroke	3.50x4.25 in.
Displacement	82 cu. in.
BHP	55 (net)
Gearbox	4 speeds
Shift	left foot
Wheelbase	66.3 in.
Wheels	21F/16R
Suspension	telescopic forks, swing-arm rear
Weight	652.5 lb. (curb)
Seat height	26 in.
MPG	47
Top speed	110 mph (est.)

Worth checking out, as they say in the Texas movie reviews.

Three stars: The other early models

Hard lines. Nor do I wish to criticize. A solid FXE or the newer Wide Glide, Fat Bob and so on can be worth having. My own personal favorite, in terms of good looks and easy operation, was the single-tank FX of 1973. There are lots of early Super Glides out there, and you can find a good one for $2,500—well, I've seen them and I never get to the real bargains on time.

Mostly, they combine the limited comfort of a Sportster with the bulk of an Electra Glide and make demands on their own in terms of luggage capacity and riding posture.

Further, the newer FXR line has equal style with a better drivetrain. The average Super Glide is just that—average.

Three point five stars: The Softails

The original Softail was a tremendous success and the expansion of the theme has done wonders for the sales chart. One can also assume the bikes have made many people happy.

But I must advise caution at this point.

Value is in the collective eyes of those who wish to behold. The Softails sold well in large part because they were new and different and there was a styling change every year or more often. And of course it's fun to have a new machine that looks like an old one.

Problem is, a whole bunch of riders interested in style leaped into the hobby at a time when there were so many variations it's hard to keep track without a chart: I did in fact wind up making a chart so's I'd know what was what.

Several years down the road, I suspect we'll have a flock of used motorcycles that look older than they are, while the fashion will have become something else. One of my sons bought a Fat Boy and paid full pop because it was new, and another son picked up a Springer at a bargain because the original owner had more toys than he could play with.

The Softails are fun. But I don't expect they'll be what you could really call an investment.

Chapter 3

★★★	FXR 1982-86

FXR Series

Early in 1981, designated tipsters at Harley-Davidson began hinting about a new machine, something along the lines of a stripped FLT Tour Glide. Some months later, when the FXR line was formally introduced, its all-inclusive title was Super Glide II.

Evidently not even the guys at the factory really appreciated the importance or the progress of what they'd done. The FXR series was not just a stripped FLT, not merely a different FXE. One could instead say the total was more than the sum of the parts.

The 1982 FXRS was much different than it looked. Note the rearward shocks and triangulated frame tubes behind the engine. Steve Broaddus photo.

The project did begin with the FLT's three-point suspension mounts for the drive-train. That system worked so well on the big bike the engineers thought they'd extend the idea, use it for a smaller machine. But when they'd stripped the permanent fairing and saddlebags from an FLT, the result looked sort of nekkid, with the odd suspension extended out front and lots of wasted space in the back. And because this was to be a lighter machine, the different front end wasn't needed.

So the designers went the full distance. They (and the computer) did a new frame, for the 80 in. engine and five-speed gearbox and insulating mounts, but with an FX- or XL-style front end and the overall appearance of the Super Glide. Thus the new model was more than either of the designs on which it was based.

The first year

The Super Glide II designation disappeared almost immediately, replaced with FXR-based letters and with different names, such as Low Glide, Sport Glide or Disc Glide.

That first year there were two models and no names. There was the FXR, with wire wheels and one-tone paint, and the FXRS with cast wheels and Dunlop Sport Elite tubeless tires, a small sissy bar, highway pegs and contrasting panels on the tank.

FXR had a single tank, with fuel gauge on the console and tach, speedo and warning lights on the top clamp. *Road Rider* photo.

Both were an immediate hit. One factor was that the 1982 Shovelhead engine came with lower compression ratio and ran better on regular gas, plus it had an oil control package, with extra drain lines from heads to crankcase, and better valve guides and seals. Magazines that hadn't been paying attention to Harley suddenly did, and they commented about how much cleaner and smoother these new models were compared to what they'd last seen.

The FXR frame was five times stiffer in torsion than the FX frame. The older version had the rear shocks up close to the seat, which took up space and put extra strain on the swing arm because the shock was mounted at the middle of the arm while the axle was at the end. The incoming force had twice the leverage of the point that resisted it. The new frame was better braced at the rear

The new frame let the FXR be as narrow as it looks here. The highway pegs and windshield were factory-offered accessories. *Road Rider* photo.

and extended back to just about the rear axle, so the shock got what the axle gave it, not twice as much. Moving the shocks back freed space for the oil tank and battery to be within the frame rails, effectively narrowing the center of the bike.

Cycle World's certified scales said the FXRS with 4.2 gal. tank half full weighed 605 lb., lighter than the FX models were then. The FXRS turned the standing quarter mile in 14.26 sec. at 91 mph, hit 99 mph in the flying half mile and returned 50 mpg. Oil usage was 1,500 mpqt., just what the factory predicted. The testers said the suspension and controls were stiff but effective, handling was fine and the upright posture on the stepped seat wasn't as bad as it used to be.

Model year 1983

The FXR and FXRS were carried over for 1983, joined by a new model, the FXRT. The T was for Touring except Harley couldn't call it that in name, what with the Tour Glide already on the market, so it's come to be called the Sport Glide.

By this time Harley-Davidson was owned by its managers and they were aware that they weren't getting all the buyers they wanted. The FLT was larger than the average Japanese motorcycle and it looked it.

So the product planners put the FXRT into the mainstream. It had a frame-mounted fairing styled along conventional lines, ditto for the saddlebags. Rear drive was by enclosed chain, as seen on the FLT. (At the time, the toothed belt drive and the five-speed gearbox were too wide to fit into the same frame at the same time.) The FXRT had air-adjustable rear suspension and air-controlled antidive on the forks: When the front brakes were applied a valve closed a reserve chamber linked to the fork tubes. Air volume was reduced, so the pressure went up and the front end resisted diving down. It worked, too.

Flip-up seat concealed the centralized oil tank and battery of the newly framed FXR. *Road Rider* photo.

Sorry about the poetry; the guy who parked the bike there comes from Havahd Yahd. Anyway, the FXRT had fairing and saddlebags styled like the others on the market. *Road Rider* photo.

The FXRT took some getting used to, in the sense that dealers and hardcore buyers didn't think it looked enough like a Harley, while non-Harley prospects weren't yet sure that it didn't look too much like those bikes nice people aren't seen on. And they were worried about all they'd heard about quality control. (That's been taken care of. All the magazines are now struggling with telling the public how good the domestic product has become, while not sounding like captives of the sales department.)

The FXRT did look good in the tests. *Road Rider* quoted the factory's claim of 640 lb. dry, while *Cycle World*'s observed test weight was 668 lb., fuel aboard; the added pounds were, of course, the fairing and bags.

The fairing shielded the test riders and passengers and made them more comfortable in the seat for more hours. *Cycle World* clocked an honest 101 mph and 47 mpg, so the fairing—remember, same engine as the FXRS—reduced air drag. *Cycle World* got through its 4,000 mile test without adding oil. *Road Rider*'s example did 1,500 mpqt. The testers added that the crankcase breather was feeding oil into the airbox, from whence it dripped. Installing a new air filter and resealing the box didn't cure this, so it's something to watch for.

The 1983 FXRT used an enclosed chain, like the FLT. *Road Rider* photo.

Model year 1984

FXR models began the 1984 year with the V2 engine, a major step as noted earlier in this treatise. Not to repeat too much, the V2 goes as far as it can toward being a new engine in the original configuration. It's lighter, cleaner, stronger and more efficient and powerful than the Shovelhead was.

Take notes here because the names can befog. The FXRT was billed as the Sport Glide, for reasons mentioned. What we might think was the Sport Glide, the FXRS, was named the Low Glide. (This isn't the best moniker, although I can't right now come up with a better one. The sales department picked the name; it didn't worry about confusing the Low Glide with either the Low Rider or the Super Glide, both of which used a different frame and, for part of 1984, at least, a different engine.

Saddlebags for FXRT came with liners, in case of rain or a nearby laundromat. *Road Rider* photo.

The sales department was worried about seat height, an advertised figure that (to me) is given more importance than it deserves. True, people like to plant their feet on the showroom floor but what really matters when riding is width of the seat and frame and location of the pegs, all of which mean as much as what the ruler says.

But the sales people persuaded the factory to lower the FXRS for 1984. The shocks and forks were shortened. They then had to be stiffer because they had the same loadings to handle with less wheel travel. The ride of the 1984 FXRS was rougher than the first version, plus having pegs and pipes closer to the ground meant it was easier to drag them under hard cornering.

At any rate the bike was lowered, the ad guys made much of it and the magazines didn't like it. Sales went up, though, which should teach me something.

The 1984 limited edition was the FXRDG, the Disc Glide. It was an FXRS with an alloy wheel, a solid one, in back. And it had some nifty paint, in particular a tank emblem that read Genuine Harley-Davidson, with the first letter in tastefully ornate script. If that

Year and model	1984 FXRT (Sport Glide)
Engine	ohv 45° V-twin
Bore and stroke	3.50x4.25 in.
Displacement	82 cu. in.
BHP	55 (net)
Gearbox	5 speeds
Shift	left foot
Wheelbase	64.7 in.
Wheels	19F/16R
Suspension	telescopic forks, swing-arm rear
Weight	658 lb. (curb)
Seat height	29.7 in.
MPG	48
Top speed	100 mph (est.)

V2 engine, here in a 1984 FXRDG, showed its heritage but was a neater, more streamlined package. Chromed covers on everything were part of the model. Scott Darough photo.

The RS version came with contrasting paint on the tank, and a small sissy bar. This is a 1984, the lower one. Buzz Buzzelli photo.

HARLEY-
DAVIDSON

sounds tongue in cheek, it's my fault. I liked the looks and kept one for as long as I could.

The real 1984 change was the diaphragm spring clutch, fitted to all the V2 models during the model year. It gave more grip for less effort at the lever, making shifting the Harleys just like shifting an ordinary motorcycle, for the first time in the big twin's long history. (Okay, when shift was hand and clutch was foot, Harley and Indian shifted alike except different hand. I mean lately.)

Model year 1985

The diaphragm spring clutch and its attendant sealed primary case allowed the next step, in the 1985 model year.

A motorcycle can be only so wide, and the less wide it is, the better. When the belt final drive and the five-speed gearbox arrived separately, it was because there wasn't room for them both at the same time. But for 1985 the new primary case was removed, so was the transmission and the starter, and the FXRs got the final belt drive which had begun earning friends in the FXB Sturgis.

There were two models in 1985, the FXRT Sport Glide and the FXRS Low Glide. The RT got a second front brake disc, a larger passenger seat, higher backrest and some graphics. Both got a new starter relay because the older one sometimes stuck.

The Low Glide was the basic model with an option, a performance package suspension. A step up, one might say, because the 1985 option was a return to the higher suspension of 1983. With more wheel travel to work with, the suspension could be softer and more comfortable and there was more cornering clearance. The optional FXRS—why it didn't have its own letters or name I don't know—also received a second disc

Disc Glide, so called because of the solid rear wheel, had a wire wheel in front for contrast, and a knock-out paint scheme. Scott Darough photo.

brake in front. All for $150, which was a bargain.

Cycle weighed the 1985 FXRS/H (for handling, my invention) at 612 lb. with full 4.2 gal. tank. Its test bike had a quarter mile elapsed time of 14.2 sec. and trap speed of 92.6 mph. Time for 0-60 mph was 5.1 sec. and average fuel use during the test was 49.6 mpg. Testers didn't record top speed or oil consumption but they did note the V2 preferred premium fuel. And they said the overall performance, the ease of operation, the reliability of the new engine, the brakes, the electrics and so forth made the FXRS "the most competent and truly versatile Harley we've ever ridden."

We'll get back to that quote but first, the limited run for 1985 was the FXRC Low Glide Custom. The C could also stand for chrome, as twelve of the various engine covers (primary drive, rocker box, cam gear, transmission top and side) were chrome plated. Not easy when most of the parts were aluminum. Paint for the special model was candy orange with root beer trim (again, it looks better than it sounds). It had 16 in. rear wheel, 19 in. front, both wire spokes, and the front wheel was covered with an XR1000 fender.

The factory announced it would only make 1,075 examples, plus a handful of FLTs and FLHTs with the chromed engine parts.

Also rare but different are the police models of the FXRT. Harley was pushed out of the police business some time back but got serious and built special models, then went after the orders. The company's best cus-

The Custom FXRS for 1985 was this C model, painted in candy orange and root beer, set off with chromed covers everywhere.

Basic 1985 FXRS had one front disc, no sissy bar but kept the contrasting paint from before. This is the low one. The higher one, the better handler and rider, also got a second front brake. If you have the choice, get the latter. Harley-Davidson photo.

Fairing and bags on the FXRT made the touring model look like the competition. Rearward passenger position meant you couldn't use a big box, and the seat itself was skimpier than the armchair on an FLT. Sport touring is the term. Harley-Davidson photo.

Year and model	1985 FXRS (Low Glide)
Engine	ohv 45° V-twin
Bore and stroke	3.50x4.25 in.
Displacement	82 cu. in.
BHP	55 (net)
Gearbox	5 speeds
Shift	left foot
Wheelbase	64.7 in.
Wheels	19F/16R
Suspension	telescopic forks, swing-arm rear
Weight	612 lb. (curb)
Seat height	29.5 in.
MPG	50
Top speed	100 mph (est.)

tomer so far has been the California Highway Patrol. The police bikes are not much different, except they have solo seats and racks and brackets for the radio and such. Police departments trade in after a set time or mileage and usually the machines have been cared for because the motor officers are volunteers, take their bikes home at night and fix the little things.

Model year 1986

A more evolved form of evolution was displayed for 1986. Federal controls became more stringent so all the Harleys got new intake and exhaust systems, for less noise. They all got turn signals that could be set either to blink when the button was held down, the old way, or to blink until the switch was turned off, the way all the other factories did it.

The entry-level big twin was the FXR Super Glide. Most 1985 buyers wanted the stiffer suspension option on the FXRS, so that became the standard fitting for 1986. Because the name itself was popular, the Low Rider tag was given to the FXRS when the old-style FXB was dropped. Yes, the FXRS was higher

Shades of yesteryear, the cops are back on Harleys! The FXRT/P kept the fairing but replaced the bags and passenger with radio and other gear. The solo seat would be worth having if you like long days and don't want company. Harley-Davidson photo.

than before, but people liked the name more than they cared about the facts.

In the same vein the FXRT, T for Touring, was called the Sport Glide, despite the standard frame-mount fairing and saddlebags. The closest 1986 to a special edition was the Liberty Edition (as in Statue of Liberty) paint and graphics offered for the FXRT.

The Grand Touring R-type was the FXRD; the T with a top box and 40-watt stereo sound system, which also came as an FXRT option.

Model Year 1987

Here's a nifty touch. The FXR line, the Rubber Glides, have always been better machines than the rigid-mount FXs. The chopper look, Customs as the trade press calls them, makes the headlines and draws the crowds.

So for 1987 H-D combined the two. Starting point was the new and excellent FXR chassis and suspension, with the normal V2 engine, five speed and belt final drive. The year's new model had the 21 in. spoked front wheel, with a solid disc rear wheel, as first seen with the Disc Glide, the small headlight from the XL and FX line, chrome and black powertrain, and various extra trim bits. All the good new engineering with the style of the day. As the press office said, the Low Rider Custom FXLR would appeal to those who liked the original look and wanted the improvements. Once again, it worked.

Elsewhere in the line the FXRT got a better sound system because it had to fill in for the discontinued FXRD Grand Touring model, which didn't sell and was dropped. All the FXRs now came with belt final drive,

The 1986 entry-level big twin, in Harley's terms, was the FXR Super Glide (because there were no plain FX-style models, they didn't need to use the II any more). The FXR's seat was half an inch lower than that of the FXRS Low Rider and it was the only big twin with chain final drive. All the R-models had a sight gauge and a relocated (neater) drain for the oil tank. Harley-Davidson photo.

meaning no more chains for the big twins, and all the FXRs except the full-fendered FXRT now were fitted with the XR-1000's small front fender.

Model Year 1989

No, we didn't forget 1988. Instead, there were no new models that year.

In 1989 the FXRs got another logical improvement, with the Low Rider Convertible.

Clever: Take the basic FXR and add saddlebags, actually semi-soft leather bags across the rear fender, and a Lexan windshield. Attach both with quick-release fittings so you got a sport bike for daily driving or Sunday in the mountains and a touring bike for summer vacation. The Convertible had highway pegs and a sissy bar and a good selection of solid and two-tone paint schemes and it filled another niche in the line-up.

Model Year 1991

Yep, another leap as the FXRs sailed through 1990 with shared improvements like the new clutch and different carburetor common to all the big twins.

In 1991, though, another major change:

The name was Sturgis, chosen to celebrate the 10th anniversary of the first Harley by that name and the 50th anniversary of the South Dakota get-together that in 1991 made the world news because literally hundreds of thousands of bikers showed up for the occasion: Yup, me too and all I wanna say about that is, it's possible for even me to get tired of straight pipes through the night.

The new Sturgis, quoting *Cycle*, was "the most significant Harley to come out in almost a decade."

This was so because of still another engineering breakthrough/extension.

The original Rubber Glide system needed a wraparound frame and lots of room for the engine/gearbox/swing arm to move around in while taking up the vibrations.

The Sturgis used an improved version, with two fewer mounts, less space to shake in and a stiffer and tighter frame, one that didn't need to extend beyond the rest of the drivetrain. Not needing to re-invent the wheel, as *Cycle* phrased it, the designers used the V2 engine and five speed and belt drive, cast wheels and so forth.

There were some concessions to form, as in a longer wheelbase: The Sturgis was a Custom, a factory chopper, and it had to have that aspect. The length let the oil tank go behind the engine rather than aft and above, which eliminated the exterior oil lines. By tipping the engine back four degrees it could be moved forward, for a lower steering head and more stability at speed. There was one disc brake in back and only one in front, a sign, *Cycle* was told, that the Sturgis wasn't a sport bike.

Which it wasn't, not quite. It was fractions longer and lower than the FXR Sport, for instance, and the cruiser controls' position sat the rider up higher than was comfortable faster than 60 mph. *Cycle*'s example weighed 627 lb. with full tank, did the quarter mile in 13.58 sec. and returned 39 mpg in daily/testing use.

What the figures don't show is how clearly the improvements came through. Every function was more, well, functional. It's awkward when you write tests sometimes because first, you were the man who said the FXR was perfectly smooth and now you're the same guy but the new model is better than the one that was perfect and it sounds like hype.

In the case of the Sturgis, it was fact, a clear, major gain in comparison with the earlier isolated mounts as well as the rigid mounts for the big twins and the XLs.

As extras, the ugly crossover pipe that for legal/noise reasons must connect the two exhaust pipes was tucked out of sight and painted black, while a Harley finally got a real fork lock instead of two holes for your own padlock.

The new Sturgis, lettered FXDB to represent the Super Glide plus Dyna Glide chassis plus B to recognize the first Sturgis which was lettered FXB, B in that example meaning Belt drive, was a superior machine in itself. It was a limited edition, all of which sold out, and in engineering terms one can say that Dyna Glide could be justified as a new line, as new as the original Super Glide was.

HARLEY-
DAVIDSON

Low Rider Custom took the solid rear wheel and laced 21 in. front wheel from the Custom line and combined them with the absorbent mounts and belt drive of the obviously modern FXRs. Look cool and ride easy, was the motto. Harley-Davidson photo.

The CONV in the FXRS-CONV designation is because the windshield and bags come off quickly and easily, so the model converts back and forth from sport bike to touring bike. Good idea, although sales haven't lived up to expectations. Harley-Davidson photo.

The rest of the FXR line was mostly unchanged, as the six lesser machines got self-canceling turn signals, upgraded tires and added color options.

Model Year 1992

Playing to strength, the 1991 Cycle Week at Daytona Beach, the 50th anniversary of the races there, was used to introduce the second Dyna Glide, the FXDB Daytona, as H-D's first 1992 model. It was also a limited edition and again, the actual 1,700 examples weren't released for sale until August 1991, when the rest of the 1992 models were announced.

The Daytona had the same frame, engine mounts and so forth, but got a second front brake (which didn't make it a sport bike, by the way) and had buckhorn bars. Where the Sturgis used black, the Daytona had chrome trim with two-tone Indigo Blue and Gold Pearlglo, quoting the maker, paint.

The marketing department must have used some muscle because there was a second Dyna Glide in 1992. It was the FXDC, Super Glide Dyna chassis with C for custom and was mechanically identical to the Daytona. The trim and paint were monochromatic, two-tone silver and black, with unpainted aluminum powertrain with chrome covers where practical. The FXDC wasn't intended to be limited, but by this time Harleys were so popular most of the models were sold out before the end of the model year.

The other FXRs, now named Low Riders instead of Super Glides by the way, carried over except for recalibrated carburetors, new oil lines and pump cover, improved brake disc material and a new belt sprocket retainer "to ensure that the drive sprocket nut stays tight for the life of the vehicle." Don't that

The Sturgis introduced Harley-Davidson's next generation. It was the debut of the computer-designed frame and mounting system, which uses less space and fewer parts than the original Rubber Glide design. The components were stretched out, lowered and then collected into a crouching, muscular package, as timely as the first FX was 20 years earlier. Harley-Davidson photo.

make you feel good about your pre-'92 belt drive?

Some Guesswork

The Dyna Glide chassis is the first H-D work to be done with computer help and under the control of management that really cared about the product and the long-term future.

The superior mounting system for the engine and the better and more compact frame used for the Dyna Glides could be easily adapted—or so it seems from the outside—for the FXRs, the FLTs and, yes, even the Sportsters.

My guess, and I haven't bothered to even hint about this with those who know, is that the Dyna Glides are the Harleys of the future.

What to look for

We've come one heck of a long way with the big twins, not just in years. As with the factory, we're dealing here with modern motorcycles, not old machines that appeal only to the home craftsman or collector.

So we can skip the part about how the heads from this year fit the cylinders from that year. Mostly, the V2 and Shovelhead parts don't swap and while you could, in theory, put a V2 engine in a Shovelhead frame, or retrofit the diaphragm spring clutch instead of the coil spring clutch, it wouldn't be worth it.

With the FXR series, we have a consistent trend. The newer ones are better than the older ones, possibly excepting the 1984 FXRS and its predecessor.

Nor are there many used FXRs on the market, not yet. Their condition will be virtually identical, assuming no crash damage or plain neglect.

The problems are mostly shared problems. Be careful to check the plug from alternator to regulator, which works loose despite several design changes. And look for,

Black on black made the Sturgis even more dramatic. Power train is the normal 80 ci big twin, with five speeds and belt drive. The oil tank is tucked in behind the engine next to the gearbox, though, and the space beneath the seat where the tank used to be now houses electrical gear. Harley-Davidson photo.

FXDB Daytona was the second Dyno Glide; the DB doesn't stand for Daytona Beach. It was a variation on the Sturgis, with the same chassis, suspension and powertrain but with two-tone paint, buckhorn bars and a second front disc brake. Harley-Davidson photo.

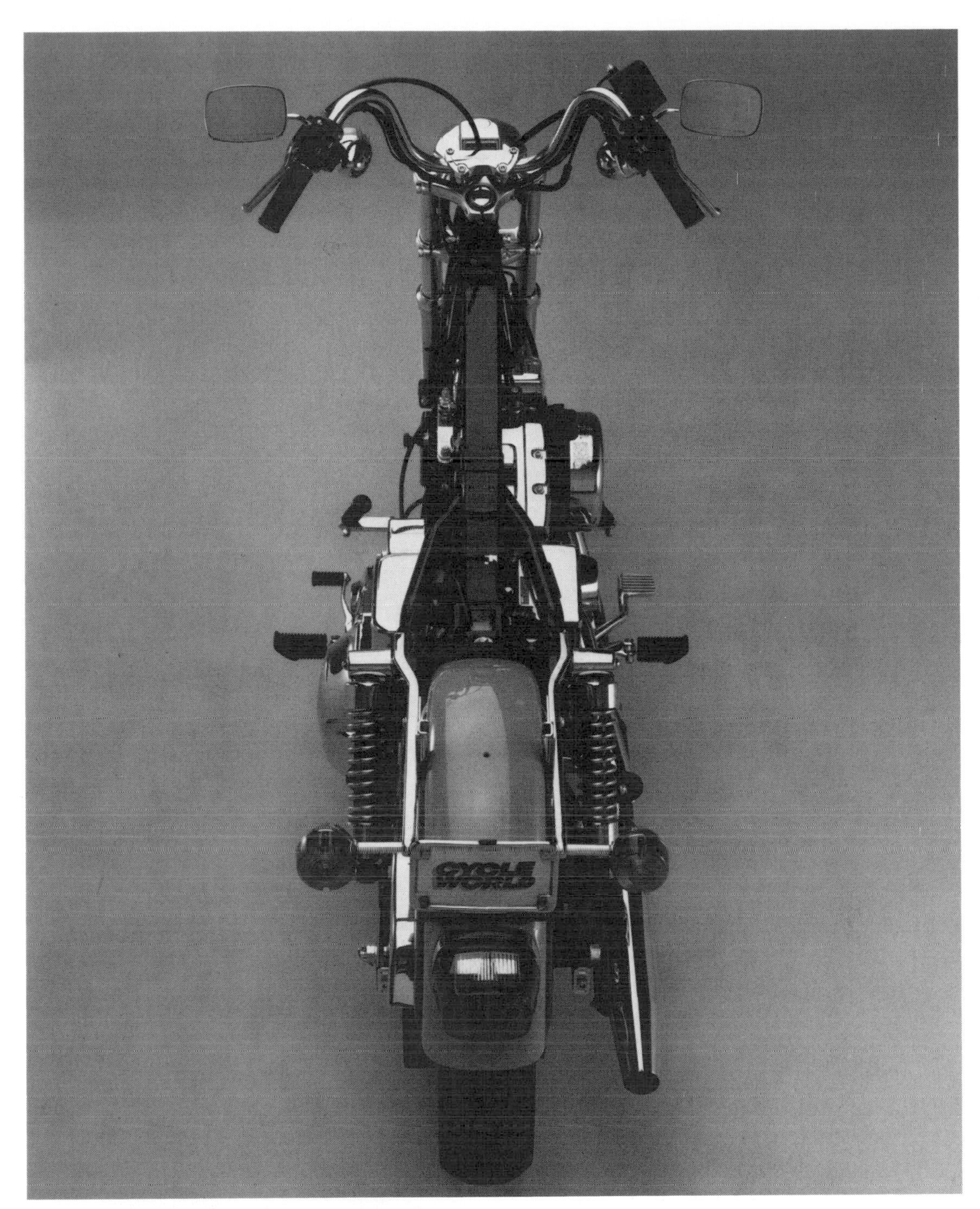

The Dyna Glide frame had a massive square backbone. The factory called this an "internal" frame because the tubes were tucked out of sight wherever possible. *Cycle World*

but don't despair at, oil seeping from airbox, primary cover or breather.

There were some random engine failures during 1982 and 1983, with no reason given. Fortunately there haven't been any lately and, anyway, if the engine was going to have a random flaw, it would have shown up by now. The starter relay gave trouble until the new one was fitted in 1985 but if the early version gives out, it can be replaced with the later one.

The Keihin carburetor used on the big twins since 1980 sometimes comes with accelerator pump jets improperly aimed. Remove the air cleaner, whack the throttle full open and watch where the fuel stream goes. If it doesn't go to both sides equally, it needs alignment. Post-1980 carbs have less accelerator pump capacity than earlier ones and your engine may run too lean at idle, but because of federal or local regulations, these are fixes you'll have to pursue yourself.

Other than the above, every year has been better than the year before it.

Ratings: Four for the best . . .

The Sturgis, Daytona and Dyna Glide Custom are still new models at this writing, so this is a prediction rather than a report . . . but even so, they will be worth having in the future.

Sport Glide FXRD Grand Touring Edition topped the 1986 R-model line, with fairing, saddlebags, top box and a 40-watt stereo sound system all part of the package. The RD also had a 2-into-1 exhaust system rather than staggered duals, and came with floorboards for operator and passenger. The seat was thicker and there were guards for bags and engine. The F-series engine got still another revision to the starting system; the relay was removed and the factory said that upped cranking power by 10 percent. This hints at problems in 1985, although there haven't been any rumors about them. Harley-Davidson photo.

Dyna Glide oil tank was located above the gearbox. It was less likely to sump and the underseat space could be used for electrical components. *Cycle World*

One reason is that the Sturgis especially is the first of the new line and like the first FX, sets a style. Being limited in production doesn't hurt, either.

Mostly though, the early Dyna Glides are worth keeping if you have one and worth getting if you find one because they are really good machines. There are fans now who want 'em and can't get 'em, which means they will appreciate.

Might add here that so far I've only seen one Sturgis for sale used. The asking price was only a bit more than the list price new.

. . . And three stars for the rest

Three stars is average and that may seem to conflict with the praise given the FXRs of all description.

It's not a contradiction to say that the newest and best mechanical designs from Milwaukee will be average investments. Rather, it's a tribute to the buyers.

The FXRs aren't going to be discovered. Their merits are established. They have been in demand since new. That's good news for the original buyer and means that the next owner will pay a little more. Free market and all that.

Personal preference will play a big part here. An FXRT will have more room for luggage than the plain FXR, less than an FLT. You get a sleeker look with the lower FXR, better handling and brakes with the Sport version, and so it will go through the line. The newer models will be worth more than the older ones because they have better designs and fewer miles. Belts are better than chains, Evo engines are better than Shovels. You'll get what you pay for, with the only exception I can think of being that because the Sturgis and Daytona will command extra dollars, the plain FXR Sport may be a better deal, especially if you really would rather have Sport than Looks.

New mounting system controlled drivetrain shake in half the space, so the engine, frame, tank, seat and so forth could all be closer to each other. *Cycle World*

Chapter 4

Sports and Sportsters

★★★ + K series, KH, KHK 1952-56
★★★★ Kick-start 883 1957-67
★★★★ XLCH with fiberglass 1970
? V2 Evolution 883, 1100 1985-86
★★★ All others

The K series, 1952-56

Among the many other things war inflicts on the world, it allows lots of people to visit new places and see new and different things, while those at home get to think.

In the case of motorcycles and World War II, Americans went everywhere in the world and they saw, among other items not pertinent here, other motorcycles. Some of the foreigners were pretty good machines; consequently the imported motorcycle went from a rarity to an option, with British Triumphs, BSAs, Nortons et al becoming what many bike nuts bought instead of a Harley or an Indian.

This wasn't lost on the guys at Harley-Davidson, who while engaged in war work had been thinking about updating their civilian products. Thus, as soon as peace returned Harley phased out the old flathead 74 and 80 twins in favor of the ohv 61 and 74, and brought out the company's first two-stroke.

But the major impact, then until now, was Harley's first modern motorcycle since the E of 1936. Its name was K. (I know, that's not a name, it's a letter. But H-D didn't use names then.) The letter was in the factory's family sequence, as it followed the J and JD from thirty years earlier and replaced the W series in engine size.

The K was lots of new stuff at once. The clutch was controlled by the left hand, the gearshift by the right foot. Front suspension was telescopic tubes and rear suspension was trailing (swing) arm with coil-over shocks—pretty much the description of motorcycle suspension today.

The engine was semi-modern. It was a 45° V-twin, naturally. But while the larger Harley twins had separate engine and gearbox, the K had what's known as unit construction; the crankcase and gearbox were in one package, two sides that bolted together. The flywheels, one left and one right, joined by a crankpin, were at the front center of the unit. The crankpin carried fork and blade connecting rods, one inside the other so the cylinders were in line fore and aft. The primary case was on the left, with a chain from engine sprocket to clutch and mainshaft sprocket. On the right was the timing case, containing four one-lobe camshafts in a row, with a gear on the shaft from the right flywheel driving the cams, the ignition timer, the oil pump below the case and the generator at the case front and below the front cylinder.

Bore and stroke were 2.75 by 3.8125 in., the same as the W-series engine that preceded the K. The K engine was semi-modern because it was a side valve, a flathead, with valves and ports part of the cylinder itself rather than over the cylinder in the head.

From the viewpoint of today, what with double overhead camshafts and multiple cylinders and competition to see how many valves can be crammed into the combustion chamber, it's easy to question Harley's reluctance to quit making flatheads.

But then, it made sense. Harley-Davidson knew a lot about flatheads, had been making good ones for decades while at that time still struggling with controlling oil on the ohv twins.

Second, while side valves look hopelessly outmoded now, Ford and Plymouth managed to flog their postwar flathead models; there were even waiting lists for them. And if the Brits had overhead valves, they were still using separate engines and gearboxes when Harley had gone to unit construction.

Having said all that, the K still comes across as only a modest success. Ready to go, a K weighed about 400 lb. and had about 30 bhp. It came with a lovely 4.5 gal. tank, 3.25x19 in. wheels, drum brakes and a choice of solo or dual seat. It was a good-looking bike.

But it wasn't especially fast. Magazines of the day were shy about actually subjecting motorcycles to merciless clocks, so there aren't many timed reports. But the K would hit about 80 mph flat out, and it strained under the weight of a second occupant. The BSA and Triumph crowds could outrun the K with their 500 cc ohv twins, and K sales weren't what the factory had hoped for. For the inside few, there was a partial answer.

By no coincidence, national championship races then were run for production-based machines limited to 750 cc, the displacement of the sporting Harleys and Indians. When the K replaced the W, Harley's racing department replaced the WR with the KR. The KR was a flathead 750 that looked like the K on the outside but was different on the inside (hot cams, detailed attention to the valves and valvetrain, choice of gears and so on). The KR used ball bearings for less friction, where the K had roller bearings or bushings.

The factory combined the K with the KR, and came up with the KK—road gear, roller bearings in the engine but hot cams, polished

The original Model K of 1952 looks so familiar now because much of it lives on with the Sportster. When new, the telescopic front suspension and swing arm rear suspension and foot shift/hand clutch were radically new. The carburetor was on the bike's left side with the intake manifold routed between the cylinders. Harley-Davidson photo.

ports and all the racing stuff that worked on the street. It was supposed to have been fast. Hard to tell because I've not found any published reports, nor does the model appear in the factory's official history. I'd say few enjoyed this model because I suspect only a handful were built and the dealers or private racers got them.

KH and KHK, 1954-56

A more practical cure for lack of power appeared in 1954, with the KH. "There's no substitute for cubic inches," the hot rodders used to say, and generally they're right. The KH had the K's bore but the stroke was lengthened to 4.5625 in., which is long.

Displacement increased from 750 cc (45 cu. in.) to 883 cc (54 cu. in.). Nor was that all: The KH had new flywheels, higher barrels, a new clutch, bigger valves and an improved transmission.

Cycle magazine tested the 1954 KH and said it was two seconds quicker through the quarter mile than the K, at 14.75 sec. It was clocked at 95 mph and got 41 mpg, which wasn't at all bad. So the KH was close to

A genuine KHK, courtesy of owner Len Andres. Note that it looks just like the plain K; all differences are internal and that makes it hard to authenticate. Note also the right-side shift lever. Harley big twins shifted on the left, by hand or foot. One can guess now that the K (and later the Sportster) shifted on the right because the competition from England did.

matching the English competition but, again, it didn't set any sales records.

The sporting model was the KHK, legend of my youth. As the letters hint, the KHK was a combination of KK and KH; it had the hot cams and polished ports but also all the road equipment and the more durable roller bearing lower end.

The KHK was offered to the public. According to the records, in 1956 the KHK outsold the KH, 714 to 539. (You see my point about sales records.) Legend says the KHKs and KKs were assembled by the racing shop, but while a few hundred examples isn't much in sales terms, it's one heck of a lot for the racing team to bolt together between weekends. More likely the parts came from the racing shop and the machines were assembled in the usual way.

At any rate, the KH was something of an interim model because the factory had the Sportster on the drawing boards.

Year and model	1954 KH
Engine	side valve, 45° V-twin
Bore and stroke	2.75x4.56 in.
Displacement	54 cu. in.
BHP	38 (claimed)
Gearbox	4 speeds
Shift	right foot
Wheelbase	n/a
Wheels	19F/18R
Suspension	telescopic forks, swing-arm rear
Weight	n/a
Seat height	n/a
MPG	41
Top speed	100 mph (observed)

What to look for

Several problems here. The K and KH had the smallest production runs of any road machine in this book. So, while mechanical parts were shared between them, and to some degree with the later Sportster, to say that a determined owner can get his motor running isn't to say it will be authentic.

Multiply that. Literally generations of owners have been modifying and adding and subtracting and making do with the K and KH for thirty years. The bikes came from the factory with different seats and bars and so forth, and all the bits have been passed back

A set of used flywheels for a K model. This is the left side. The roller main bearing shows it's a K engine; the racing KR had ball bearing mains, while the KH had a longer stroke. These flywheels can be rebuilt, but only by experts.

Consider this challenge: nonrunning K model, as offered for sale at a swap meet; no carb, no lights and no knowing what the engine was like inside. No knowing the price either; I hung around all day but couldn't find the owner. David Gooley photo.

and forth. The K or KH is easy to make do with, but difficult to get right.

Double that for the KK and KHK. Because they began as modified versions of the stock model, the performance-optioned bikes can be replicated by private owners, and they have been. The KK and KHK are legends. There must be thousands of enthusiasts who heard the stories but never actually saw one of the machines. You see the problem. I for one can vouch for only one genuine KHK in the world and I can do that only because the present owner, dealer Len Andres, sold it new and bought it back. (Sorry, he intends to keep it.)

Not every part is in the specialist catalogs. And the specialists say there isn't much demand for the parts they have, never mind tooling up to make replacements that they don't have.

Your starting point will be to identify what you find on the market. The cases shouldn't be a problem, as they are stamped; well, the left half is stamped just below and between where the barrels bolt on, with K or KH as the case (sorry) might be, and the year. Most K parts won't work with KH parts, while many KH parts can be replaced with Sportster parts, but the details are too complicated to go into here. Suffice it to say that you can build one from baskets, but don't do it if you can avoid it.

Frames have no numbers, ditto for the various other parts, although most of them (brakes, tanks and so on) can be used without undue mechanical revision.

What you really must do here is be sure. If it isn't stamped KHK, it isn't one.

Past that hurdle, though, the K and KH were underpowered so they don't put the parts to extra stress. The first ('52 and '53) engines had the transmission inside the cases and it was weak. Later engines had a trap door so the gears could come out with the cases intact and the engine in the frame—so 1954 and later is better.

The electrics were 6 volt and the lights weren't dazzling. The generator gave trou-

First-year (1957) Sportster was plain XL, obviously based on the KH with FL influence, as in the covers for the top clamp, the post for the seat and the two pipes feeding one muffler. Harley-Davidson photo.

ble—*all* Harley generators give trouble—likewise the regulator. You can get a kit and use a VW generator and a Bosch regulator or a solid state one from Voltpak.

The rear suspension was mushy. The clutch was supposed to run dry, while living in the primary case along with the primary chain and oil from the gearbox that was there to lubricate the primary chain. Unless the clutch cover gasket and seal were perfect, oil got into the clutch and it slipped or locked solid or both.

If you'll be riding the bike rather than showing it, the finicky Linkert carburetor can be replaced with a slide-valve, easily tuned Mikuni.

In sum, the K and KH have no gaping flaws. Instead they have nagging little weaknesses which can be dealt with if not actually cured. If you can put up with that, the K is great fun.

Rating: Three stars plus

The essence of sound investment policy is to remember this: Dumb people buy what other people don't want. Ordinary people buy what other people want. And smart people buy what other people don't want *yet*.

The K models are a problem. On one hand, the prices are already fairly high. Asking price for a sound example at this writing is about $4,000 and one doesn't see them on the market often.

On the other hand, the demand curve doesn't seem to be rising. The smart people, the traders, are selling nonrunners for $1,500 and laughing behind their hands. They know the eager buyer is going to have more trouble finding parts than expected and they at least don't expect the rest of the world to suddenly discover the K.

Neither do I, sorry to say. One of the main motivations in collecting anything old

Early Sportsters used a cast primary cover proclaiming model name. Three bolts didn't hold it on tight enough and later covers were stamped tin, with eight bolts. Case guards, then called crash bars, were an option. Harley-Davidson photo.

is that we can buy the stuff we didn't have when we were young and poor. In my case a K was what I didn't have, so now I'd kind of like to have one.

If the profile fits, buy one—to heck with common sense. But because there are as many people selling as buying, and there's no sign of this changing, the K and KH can only be classified as having average value.

The plus in the above rating applies only to a KK or KHK. I'm not entirely sure here but because they were legends then, there's an outside chance a KK or KHK will have additional value, for show or trade. A careful four stars, then, *if you can prove the machine is what it claims to be.*

XL series, 1957-85

Serendipity, the Greek word for a happy accident, might be Harley-Davidson's middle name. The K and KH were moderately successful in that they filled a gap in the middle of Harley's model range and dealt with the newly popular imports. But they didn't sell as well as expected and they weren't as fast as they looked, while designing and tooling up for what was a very different engine had cost the company lots of money.

So Harley engineers did a logical thing. They converted the KH to overhead valves while retaining the rest of the general idea, as in unit construction, four one-lobe cams, timer atop the timing case and so on.

The engine was declared new and given the letters XL. X was the normal sequence,

This early XLH was sold new by Len Andres, bought back when the only owner retired from riding. It's perfectly stock and equipped with all options. It also shows the heritage from the KH that preceded it.

following the U and V used for the flathead big twins. L stood for higher compression (relatively speaking—the first year's engine had 7.5:1, which was higher than the KH but not really radical even back then).

The engine was in fact more different than it looked. First, although the displacement was nearly the same, listed as 883 cc or 54 cu. in., the XL had a larger bore, 3 in. compared with the 2.75 in. of the KH, and it went back to the K's stroke of 3.812 in. The bigger bore meant larger valves and the shorter stroke meant higher rpm; both meant more potential for power.

Obviously this meant new barrels and heads, cast iron, and new flywheels and cams. The new pushrods went where the valve stems used to be, up through covers to rockers pivoting in boxes/covers bolted to the heads, similar to the design used later on the big twins and known as the Shovelhead. (Note: It's possible to put the XL heads on a K or KH. Or to get a 1000-plus cc XL883 with KH flywheels. But it's not worth it.)

Harley-Davidson has ways of making you spend money. Shown here are the chrome covers for the kick-start return spring and the exhaust pipe; the lines between the pipe and the ignition timer are an optional chain oiler.

The clutch was still supposed to run dry, the oil was carried in a separate tank and the gearshift was by the right foot, just like the KH and unlike the FL.

Cycle parts were virtually identical to the KH, with telescopic forks, coil-over shocks and rear swing arm, drum brakes front and back, 6-volt electrics and starting by kick only.

By the evidence, Harley management saw the XL as a junior version of the FL. The basic Sportster—what a wonderful name!—had a solo seat, while options included dual seat, windshield, saddlebags, luggage rack and a host of add-on chrome pieces.

This made sense. Most marketing was innocent in the fifties. Racing had become something separate from street riding and the Sportster was as unfitted to the track as the KR (still in production) was tailored to it. The Sportster wasn't a superbike because they hadn't been invented yet.

The first hint of power came in 1958, when the factory upped the compression ratio of an optional engine to 9:1 and installed larger valves. This version was called the XLH, again following the system and using H as the power label.

But the real inventors of the superbike were California dealers. According to Ar-

Plastic saddlebags with guards, luggage rack and added lights were also accessories from the factory. Note the covered shocks and how they attached to short frame rails below the seat.

mando Magri, who was there, the dealers felt there was a market for a clubman bike, a stripped Sportster. The factory agreed to offer one if the dealers would order at least sixty of the things, which they did.

The 1958 versions came with magneto ignition, straight pipes, no battery and no lights. The "ugly" (Magri's word) 4.4 gal. tank was replaced with a 2.25 gal. tank—what the chopper guys called a peanut tank. And in case the buyer wanted to ride the hot rod on the road, dealers could put back the lights and muffler and a small battery for $60.

The factory's official history doesn't tell this story. But the 1958 catalog lists the XL, the XLH and the XLC. Nobody can prove that the C stands for Competition or for California. But at least it should rid us of the rumor that the CH stood for Competition Hot while the plain H was for Highway.

No matter what the name was, the model was as popular as the dealers guessed it would be. It won at the drags and in unauthorized contests of speed, and everybody wanted one. So the factory made the XLCH.

Because of the dazzling option list it's likely no two Sportsters then came off the assembly line exactly alike. But in general the XLH had the large fuel tank, double seat, ignition timer and coil, and paired exhaust pipes feeding one low muffler.

The typical XLCH had the small tank, either a short solid seat or a sprung solo seat, and magneto ignition. The XLH could have

Disregard humorous but nonstock handle on steering damper. The factory supplied brackets for the extra driving lights and windshield. Ignition switch and speedometer were in panel above headlight.

case guards; the CH could have alloy (instead of steel) wheel rims; and some of the XLCH's had high, scramble-type pipes, with pipe and separate muffler for each cylinder carried high on the right, tucked inboard.

Cycle World tested an XLCH in 1962. It had wire wheels, 18 in. rear and 19 in. front; a wheelbase of 57 in.; seat height of 30.5 in.; and weighed 480 lb. wet, which seems heavy to me. Standing-start quarter mile time was 14.3 sec. with a trap speed of 92 mph, 0-60 took 6 sec. and miles per gallon ranged between 40 and 60. Top speed was listed as 122 mph, which must have been calculated at the engine's redline rather than an actual timed run.

In 1965 *Cycle World* tested an XLH, with the same wheelbase and seat height but with 18 in. wheels at both ends and with the larger (3.75 gal.) tank. Wet weight was given as 505 lb., again higher than I expected. No top speed or miles per gallon were published. The quarter mile times were 15.5 sec. and 84 mph, with 0-60 in 7.4 sec. The times were slower than predicted, readers complained, and later published accounts from private owners gave drag strip results of 13 sec. elapsed times and trap speeds of 100 mph; possibly these were prepared to the limit of the rules.

But. Those early Sportsters were quick and fast and they could run with the imports.

There was a host of variations with the early XLs. Headlights were mounted in nacelles or from brackets that attached at the rear, the sides or the top. Sometimes the fork legs had rubber boots, sometimes not. There were solo seats with springs or solid mounts, ditto for the dual seats. At first the throttle cable was routed inside the bars, then it was moved outside. The Sportster got a 12-volt electric system in 1965 because the FL series needed it for electric start and Harley liked using one model generator for all its engines. (The gearing was different, though. Because the FL turned more slowly on the highway, its generator was geared to spin faster in relation to engine rpm.)

Year and model	1957 XL (Sportster)
Engine	ohv 45° V-twin
Bore and stroke	3.0x3.81 in.
Displacement	54 cu. in.
BHP	40 (claimed)
Gearbox	4 speeds
Shift	right foot
Wheelbase	n/a
Wheels	18 or 19 in.
Suspension	telescopic forks, swing-arm rear
Weight	n/a
Seat height	n/a
MPG	n/a
Top speed	n/a

Year and model	1962 XLCH (Sportster)
Engine	ohv 45° V-twin
Bore and stroke	3.00x3.81 in.
Displacement	54 cu. in.
BHP	55
Gearbox	4 speeds
Shift	right foot
Wheelbase	57 in.
Wheels	19F/18R
Suspension	telescopic forks, swing-arm rear
Weight	480 lb. (curb)
Seat height	30.5 in.
MPG	40 to 60
Top speed	122 mph (calculated)

The electric leg

Late in 1967 the XL cases were changed to allow installation of an electric starter. This

This 1963 XLCH has lost its front fender, has a nonstock carb and seat, but shows what a lean machine the CH was then.

was a model distinction, in that the XLH, the junior tourer, had the electric starter but the XLCH, the racing one with magneto and small tank, had only kick. But for production efficiency all the engines came with a hump in the primary case.

Cycle World testers of the 1968 XLH said the electric leg added 40 lb. to the bike's weight, but the wet weight of their example was 510 lb., so something doesn't compute: Either they changed their methods or the scales were wrong on one of the two occasions. Equally odd is that while claimed power had only gone from 55 to 58 bhp, the 1968 bike did 0-60 in 4.7 sec., the quarter mile in 13.86 sec. at 98.68 mph, and had a timed top speed of 114 mph—all much better than the 1965 test.

The CH magneto was famous for not working. (Mine, rebuilt by Joe Hunt, works flawlessly; don't give up hope.) In 1970 the CH lost its magneto in favor of the timer and coil used on the XLH. Both models had options of large or small tanks, so the only difference was the XLH starter and lower gearing for the CH, which, because of that and the presumed lower weight of the kick-only engine and smaller battery, should have been quicker.

The 1970 option was a unit seat base and rear fender, of fiberglass, much like the one that appeared later on the first Super Glide. You could still get the traditional-style fender and seat, and most buyers did.

Cycle World was becoming more discerning in its tests. Reviewers said oil consump-

Also 1963, this XLH shows how different the two models were then, despite sharing engine and frame. The gas tank was smaller and lower than on the 1957, while the speedo had been moved into the headlight nacelle. The dual seat was comfortable then, although this one needs work.

From the press kit, this shot shows the XLCH at its best, with small tank, low bars, small headlight, separate instruments and dual seat. Harley-Davidson photo.

The left side of an XLCH, parked in the Vintage pits at Daytona, 1985, shows drag-style handlebars, chromed tin cover on primary case. The odd gadget between the barrels is the horn.

An XLCH seldom stayed stock. This is an 883, my guess is 1968, with accessory seat and passenger pad. Magneto has manual control and drive for the tachometer, on the bracket behind the top clamp.

tion of the 1970 XLCH was between 250 and 500 mpqt. Their example weighed 495 lb. at the curb, with small tank and kick start only. Still, I don't know why the weight difference wasn't more, nor why those early Sportsters didn't weigh much less than the later ones.

The 1970 XLCH was easy to start, which may explain the switch from magneto to timer and coil. The mag had fixed timing and the rider obtained advance or retard by hand. The timer had built-in advance, so it was less trouble. (More late news: The magneto is separate from the rest of the electrical system, so it keeps on working when the battery goes dead, the regulator fails or the generator loses its lunch. My advice here is to stick with the system you have and learn to make it work.)

Cycle World's 1970 CH did 0-60 in 4.9 sec., the quarter mile in 14.25 at 95 mph, had a top speed of 112 mph and gave 39 mpg. That's pretty close to the earlier examples. If the first Sportsters don't show up here as lighter than the later ones, or the CH isn't markedly faster than the plain H, well, all the magazines can do is print what the clocks tell them.

The 1971 Sportsters had two major changes. One, the outside ignition timer was replaced by points and condenser behind a plate on the timing case cover. The points ran off the geartrain for the cams, generator and oil pump. The inside timer was as easy as the old one to service, and it was better isolated from water and grit and damage.

Two, the dry clutch dating back to the model K was replaced with a wet clutch.

Fiberglass rear fender and seat base were optional on 1971 Sportster, but didn't sell well. The complete machines sold this way are rare, but the bodywork itself is available at swap meets. *Cycle World* photo.

This is good news and bad news. All other factors being equal, a dry clutch is better than a wet clutch, wet meaning the plates run in oil. Oil is slippery, so to keep the clutch from slipping, wet plates need more spring pressure and that translates into extra pressure at the hand lever. Dry clutches transmit more power, more reliably, with less pressure. Almost all motorcycles use wet clutches for production bikes, dry clutches for racing.

In Harley's case (play on words there), the difficulty was that the dry clutch was inside the primary case, which contained gear lube for the primary chain. The clutch basket had a seal on the shaft side, a cover with gasket on the clutch (out)side. They didn't always work. Oil seeping into the clutch housing was a nagging problem all during its years in production, so the factory switched in 1971. The wet, post-1970 clutch had a harder lever. It's more difficult to service. But it works.

Hard lesson here. *If* you can get a good seal and install the cover perfectly, the dry clutch should stay dry and it's much nicer to use. At this writing mine is assembled with cover gasket and slops of "flexible" silicone seal, between cover and basket. It's been dry for months now, knock on wood. But most owners have taken the easy way out, with Barnett wet/dry clutch plates, Barnett racing clutch springs and ATF in the primary and gearbox. You'll have to break the plates free by rocking the bike with the transmission in gear and the clutch lever pulled in, first thing every morning. You'll never find neutral unless the bike's rolling. But the clutch won't slip under power nor lock solid when you need it to slip; both will happen if the dry clutch gets wet by accident.

Return of the 61

While Harley-Davidson was making these improvements and surviving the acquisition of the company by AMF, the motorcycle market was changing.

The Sportster was toppled from the top of the performance hill. Triumph and BSA came out with 750 cc triples and Honda stunned the world with the 750 four. They

XL-1000, circa 1973, fitted with windshield and saddlebags. *Road Rider* photo.

Watch this one. When full, the outboard oil tank could slop over if you stopped to check the level with the engine warm. *Road Rider* photo.

were faster and quicker than the 883 cc Sportster.

In 1972 Harley used the cubic inch trick. The XL engine got a bigger bore, 3.188 in. instead of 3.0. Stroke remained 3.812 in. and the displacement was rounded off to 1000 cc or 61 cu. in., same as the first ohv V-twin, the 61E of 1936.

There's not a lot of interchange between the two engines. The larger bore meant wider cylinders and a wider pattern for the bolts that held the barrels to the cases. A skilled machinist can adapt the earlier cases for the new barrels but generally it isn't worth the bother.

The 1000 cc engine (Harley wasn't to refer to it as the 61 for several years, odd for a company usually conscious of its history) was rated at 61 bhp. *Cycle World* tested a 1972 XLCH. It found the wet clutch stiffer but better than the dry one. The revised shifter drum was an improvement; the new oil pump wasn't as likely to seep oil from the tank into the sump when the bike was parked; the first three gears were closely spaced and the fourth was a long jump; the new Bendix/Zenith carb worked well; and starting was easy.

Test weight with the 2.2 gal. tank half full was 492 lb. The XL1000 did the quarter mile in 13.38 sec. at 97.7 mph, 0-60 in 5.5 sec. and topped out at 116 mph. Mileage was 43 mpg—all this with the restrictive mufflers required in California that year.

The magazine testers reported the frame wasn't especially stiff, a polite way of saying it flexed, and while this was the first Sportster they'd ride 400 miles in a day, they said the seat was "thin, narrow and uncomfortable."

That brings up another major change. The Harley people had noticed the arrival of faster machines. They'd also noticed that many customers were going the custom route, so while in 1971 the stock seat was a full dual version and the option was a skimpy pad, in 1972, production bikes came with a thin, curved seat and hardly any padding at all. The factory said it was saving time and money, giving the buyer what he wanted

An underrated model, the 1977 XLT had a thicker seat, larger tank from the FX Super Glide and saddlebags from the FLH Electra Glide. Not really valuable, but rare and worth having. *Road Rider* photo.

Drive side of XLT shows change to primary cover when a starter was fitted, and size of battery needed to spin engine. *Road Rider* photo.

instead of what he'd throw away in favor of the custom seat. Further, seat height was an advertisably low 29.3 in.

The Sportster was a big seller during this period, so the factory's move was wise.

On the other hand, the custom seat wasn't comfortable. It caused pain and discomfort and cramped the rider. The forward pegs kinked your knees while the high bars propped you into the wind. They say they made the customer happy; I say they haven't made a decent Sportster seat since 1971.

There were some other shortcomings. The frame had been revised here and there but was still mostly as it came in 1957, with cast-iron steering head and cast-iron junction at the rear of the top tube. The rear shocks were mounted on sort of a T at this rear junction and to the swing arm at mid-arm. When the electric starter was put above the gearbox aft of the rear cylinder, the oil tank and battery were crowded.

During this period the CH and plain H had different oil tanks and batteries. The H battery was awkward to service. The H oil tank was worse. It had the cap and dipstick combined, so if you checked the oil when warm the heat had expanded it and oil slopped out. Messy. And the 1972 through 1974 H models had their oil tanks near the chain. If the chain was slack and you hit a bump just wrong, the chain could saw a hole in the tank. Messy and fatal to the engine if not noticed at the time. The factory changed the tank when this was reported, but it's something to watch for.

XLH and CH got disc front brakes in 1973. In 1974 the throttles were given return

This XLCR has been customized—the exhaust pipes should be flat black. But you can see the siamese exhaust, the fairing and the extension of the frame rails so the shocks could move back and the oil tank and battery could move in, out of the way.

springs and outside cables, evidently in response to federal standards.

Those standards in 1975 required the gearshift to be by foot—which everybody was doing anyway—and on the left. In the Sportster's case (another pun, sorry), this meant using a linkage from the shift shaft on the right, back and across and forward to a new pedal on the left. The brake pedal was now on the right, working the drum rear brake.

The 1976 Sportsters were carryovers, but in 1977 H-D made two moves, noble in purpose, as Herbert Hoover said about Prohibition.

The model year began with a change to new cases that let the gearshift shaft emerge from the cases on the left, direct to the lever. And the frame was modified so the oil pump could be unbolted from the engine with the engine in the frame.

The XLH and CH were joined at the beginning of the year by the XLT, with T meaning Touring. The XLT got a 3.5 gal. gas tank, a lovely shape, from the FX Super Glide. The T had a thicker seat, lower bars and provision for windshield and saddlebags. Final drive was higher geared, for relaxed highway travel. The XLT was a Sportster to be ridden, which people may have done. What they didn't do was buy them.

Later in the year Harley introduced the XLCR, with CR standing for Cafe Racer. The engine was straight XL. The exhaust, though, began with short pipes that joined below the carb and then separated, sweeping back to separate mufflers, one on each side.

The pipes were flat black. Everything else was glossy black. There was a race-inspired 4 gal. gas tank, a race-inspired solo seat and a streamlined rear fender.

XLCR was a good answer, but the question was never asked. Willie G. Davidson used some flat-track lines, as in the rear fender and seat, and some road-race items like the small fairing, but the XLCR wasn't exactly a racer and it wasn't part of the day's fashion, that is, stock bikes that looked like mild choppers. So the XLCR didn't sell, but for some reason people expected it to become collected, and asking prices are, at this writing, still above what buyers are willing to pay, which undermines the CR's value as an investment. Harley-Davidson photo.

The frame was new. The front portion was like the other XLs but the rear was like the XR-750 racer, with triangulated top rails that extended back to above the rear axle. The CR's shocks were mounted to the rear of the swing arm, so there was room for oil tank and battery to be tucked in. The CR had rear-set footpegs, low bars and a small fairing. The cast wheels came from Morris and the all-disc brakes from Kelsey-Hayes. The XLCR had everything the road-race fan could hope for, just as the XLT was just right for the highway hauler. The XLCR didn't sell, either.

Instead, it provided progress. As a running change during 1978, all the XL models got the new frame. Some of the details were different but the rearset shocks and stiffer frame were the same in principle. All the Sportster engines got electronically triggered ignition in 1978 and the engines got the siamesed exhausts while the oil tank and battery were moved inboard for the XLCH and XLH as well as the T and CR, both of which remained in the catalog. Cast wheels were available for all and the CR could be bought with a dual seat: Why attract members of the opposite sex if you don't have a place to put them?

But Harley's weathermen were reading the sky. The XLCH hadn't really been a distinct model since the death of the magneto. The 1979 Sportsters had a new rear

The 1979 XLS, with the rear-mount shocks and new frame first seen on the 1977 XLCR. Ditto for the siamese exhaust pipes. This combination put the new rear brake master cylinder where the kick lever and exhaust used to be, which is why (1) kick start was deleted and (2) accessory exhaust pipes will often fit all XLs except the 1979. *Road Rider* photo.

master cylinder to go with the new frame and the brake system went where the kick lever used to be. Kick start was a seldom-seen option. The XLCR and XLT were dropped.

In their place was the XLS, in general an XLH but with extended forks, low bars on risers, a sissy bar with leather pouch, two-tone paint and highway pegs. It was a junior version of the FX Low Rider, and like the Low Rider, the XLS sold.

The 1980 Sportsters came in two versions, the XLH and the XLS, now named Roadster, a name picked through a contest. The XLH had optional shorter shocks, lower seat and the nickname Hugger. (Harley didn't announce the names that got second

Year and model	1972 XLCH (Sportster)
Engine	ohv 45° V-twin
Bore and stroke	3.188x3.812 in.
Displacement	61 cu. in.
BHP	61 (claimed)
Gearbox	4 speeds
Shift	right foot
Wheelbase	58.5 in.
Wheels	19F/18R
Suspension	telescopic forks, swing-arm rear
Weight	492 lb. (curb)
Seat height	29.7 in.
MPG	43
Top speed	116 mph

Year and model	1977 XLCR
Engine	ohv 45° V-twin
Bore and stroke	3.188x3.812 in.
Displacement	61 cu. in.
BHP	68 (claimed)
Gearbox	4 speeds
Shift	left foot
Wheelbase	58.5 in.
Wheels	19F/18R
Suspension	telescopic forks, swing-arm rear
Weight	515 lb., tank half full
Seat height	31 in.
MPG	44
Top speed	106 mph

First XLS (1979) had drag bars and 3 gal. fuel tank. *Road Rider* photo.

prize in this contest. It's just as well.)

In 1981 there were the XLS Roadster with buckhorn bars, shorty dual exhausts and 3.3 gal. tank, and the XLH Sportster with shorter forks and the 2.2 gal. tank. Either model came with either tank, and a choice of wire or cast wheels, with the rear wheel in 16 or 18 in. diameter.

The new(er) generation

As detailed earlier in this book, Harley-Davidson was saved (in my opinion) when it was bought by AMF, and saved again when it was bought *from* AMF by its own managers aided by several optimistic banks.

The new owners straightaway began improving the product. The 1982 Sportster got an all-new frame; that is, no more iron junctions. It was both lighter and stiffer than the one it followed. The generator produced more juice, the battery needed less care, the oil tank and battery were better positioned. Both XLH and XLS could be ordered with special trim; for example, there were decorations observing the Sportster's twenty-fifth anniversary. The engine got a thicker head gasket, dropping the compression ratio from 9:1 to 8:1, the better to cope with junk fuel. (This can be done retroactively, back through 1974, if you can't find decent gas.)

This revised Sportster was simply a better motorcycle. *Cycle World* tested a 1982 XLS and reported, bottom line first, 6,000 trouble-free miles. Because the newer bikes had more wheel travel, they were farther from the ground and wheelbase was up to 60 in. XLS seat height was only 29 in., although none of the magazine's riders really liked the seat. The test XLS weighed 515 lb. with 2.2 gal. tank half full. Too small, they said the

By 1982 the XLH was mostly style, as with the sissy bar and medium-sized tank from the Super Glide. Compare this brake master cylinder and exhaust pipe routing with that of the 1979 XLS; that's why other pipes won't fit the one year. *Road Rider* photo.

tank was; plus the air cleaner interfered with the rider's right leg and the clutch dragged. Top speed was 99 mph, elapsed time for the quarter mile was 14.26 sec. and mpg was 52.

Early in 1983 *Road Rider* testers tried a 1982 XLH, which they said was just like the 1983 version would be except they couldn't get a 1983 yet. They printed the factory's dry weight of 460 lb. Compare that with *Cycle World*'s actual weight of 515 lb. with 9 lb. of gas—perhaps the factory was a shade optimistic. The *Road Rider* people didn't clock the bike but they did measure oil usage at 700-800 mpqt., and added that although the tank was supposed to hold three gallons they could only get 2.7 out of it because the tap wasn't at the lowest part of the tank.

Next came a good marketing move. Harleys have always been expensive when compared with the Japanese machines. For 1983, Harley assembled the lightest, least-trimmed Sportster it possibly could. The bike had the standard engine and frame but came with a solo seat, peanut (2.2 gal.) tank, staggered shorty dual pipes, low bars and hardly any chrome. It was called the XLX-61, first time the company referred back to that famous figure since the XL engine grew to 1000 cc. And the XLX had a suggested retail price several hundred dollars below the other Sportsters.

Good move. Many buyers opted for extras like a passenger pad on the rear fender, but that advertised price got them into the showroom and gave them an excuse to buy, which is all you can ask a price leader to do. The XLX was quickly popular.

The second big step in 1983 was a technical and critical success even if it failed in the marketplace.

The idea began in 1972, when H-D introduced the alloy XR-750, a dirt-track engine sort of based on the iron XR750 that came from the racing XLR built out of XL883 parts. The XR750 quickly dominated AMA dirt-track racing and fans asked for a street version. Factory engineers and the people in the racing department built a few examples, prototypes even, but management said no: By the time the 750 was street legal it wouldn't have enough performance to attract buyers.

Ironically, Harley's racing 750 drove Yamaha out of AMA dirt track. Yamaha later brought out the Virago 750, which had no racing heritage and wasn't fast either, but sold like crazy. But that, too, is another story.

Anyway, some of the hotheads in the back persevered and the racing department was assigned the project of a street version of the 750. The designers used the lower end of the XL-1000 engine, topped by new iron barrels and the XR-750's alloy heads, with dual carbs at the right rear and exhausts at the left front, just like the racer's. The XR-750 had bigger bore and shorter stroke than the XL, and XR heads were taller than XL heads, so the XR-1000 had shorter connecting rods and barrels for the same overall height; that is, it fit into the stock XL frame.

This engine took plenty of hand work and money. The XR-1000 was planned as a

The traditional Sportster headlight was small, hung from a mounting bracket. It appeared on the CH, was borrowed for the Super Glide and migrated back to the other XLs. *Road Rider* photo.

limited production run. To amortize the investment the price was high—$2,000 more than for a regular XLH.

The XR-1000 was both fast and quick. *Cycle World*'s example had an elapsed time for the quarter mile of 12.88 sec., first Harley into the 12s, as the drag racers say. It had 70 bhp stock, ten up on the standard version, with at least 100 bhp available if the private owner followed the factory's booklet for tuning for off-road, ahem, use. ("May violate state law," "Kids, don't try this at home" and so forth.)

The problem was price. One could see where the $2,000 went. But those who knew Sportster engines could also see how to get more than ten more horses for much less than $2,000.

The mistake, my view here, was that all this special equipment went straight into an XLX. A good machine but the stripper of the line.

That was poor marketing. Ford and Chevrolet did a good business years ago selling Fords and Chevys with Thunderbird and Corvette engines. In fact, Thunderbirds and Corvettes came with Ford and Chevy engines; it just sounded better the other way. You can sell a low-priced version of a high-priced product better than you can sell a high-priced version of a low-priced product, especially if you have to show people the badge before they know what it is. You had to look carefully at the XR-1000 before you knew it wasn't an XLX.

Just thought I'd throw this in, to show how far one can go. The frame is accessory, the rear suspension is solid. Forks are Ceriani and I don't know where the disc wheels came from. Beneath the chrome plating and the engraving are early (pre-electric-start) 900 cases, but the timing cover is post-1970 and the kick lever comes from an FL.

If the factory had listened to me, which it didn't and never will, the XR-1000 would have come with a larger version of the XR-750 tank, a dual seat like that on the XLCR and orange and black paint like the team race bikes used.

Well, a few hundred XR-1000s were sold in 1983 and a few hundred in 1984 and there were still some in showrooms in 1985. I bet there are still people in power at H-D who think this proves people didn't want a street XR-750, while in fact we've never been offered one.

The big minor news for the 1983 Sportster line was an ignition incorporating vacuum advance that let the compression ratio be eased up to 8.8:1, a less restrictive exhaust system and a smaller air cleaner. Fine tuning got the engine within federal limits with less loss of power.

There was also change for the labels. The XLCH had disappeared, replaced by the XLX as the basic Sportster. The XLH, which used to be the fancy one, was moved into the middle with plain-topped 3.3 gal. tank and high bars. The XLS became the fancy one, with 3.8 gal. tank bearing a center console and with flat bars on risers, while the XLS lost the extended forks it had at first. The three models used the same frame, engine and mechanical parts, so tanks and bars and seats could be easily swapped.

The 1984 model year began slowly. Orange and black paint was an option for the XR-1000 (too late, see above) while the XLH, XLS and XLX got one large front disc brake instead of two smaller discs. The leverage ratios were changed to give more pressure at the disc for less at the hand lever.

Early in the fall there was a running change of epic importance: The XL series got a diaphragm spring clutch and an alternator, all in one move.

As mentioned earlier, the Sportster clutch was a problem when it was supposed to run dry. When it was changed to run in oil, it worked better but was much stiffer and required (or developed) forearms like Popeye's. During the same time, the early generators were trouble, later ones were adequate,

Late-model Sportsters were exercises in parts selection. The 1985 XLX had a solo seat, black exhaust, cast wheels, small tank and low bars. Harley-Davidson photo.

XR-1000 was an exercise in engineering and marketing. Engineering won, as the XR-1000 engine was derived from the XR-750 racer; a mix of Sportster XL-1000 lower end, new iron barrels and aluminum heads from the racing engine with dual carbs on the right, exhaust pipes on the left. The XR was fast and often won its class in the road races. But the rest of the machine was straight XLX, the bargain Sportster, and it didn't look different enough to appeal to enough customers. Those exhaust pipes are quieter than they look, by the way, and the shields keep most of the heat off the rider's left leg.

XR-1000

while the FL series alternators were flawless.

Just as youth is wasted on the young, so should everybody have to wrestle with the old clutch in order to appreciate the new one. It's so light you can just pull it in and shift. You can even get neutral when the bike is stopped. I know, it sounds simple; would that it were. The alternator is part of the clutch and the primary case was changed to give room, so while it could be done, it isn't worth it.

Model year 1985 was a year to mark time. There was the XLX, XLH and XLS. The X got black paint and a rough finish for the engine covers, the XLH had the peanut tank and the XLS kept the big tank and console while both got chrome and polish for the engines and exhaust pipes. The factory was getting ready for a surprise: the V2 Evolution Sportster.

What to look for

There are three ways to buy a used Sportster:

One, as a secondhand motorcycle to ride around on.

Two, as a restoration project.

Three, as a starting point for your very own, personal, perfect Sportster.

Starting at the top, in all its myriad forms the XL simply got better between 1957 and 1985.

This came as a surprise. Most models built for any length of time get heavier and more complicated as they become more powerful and more reliable.

But. *Cycle World* tested an XLCH in 1962 and an XLX in 1984. The 1962 had kick start and spoke wheels, the 1984 had electric start and cast wheels. They both weighed 480 lb. They both got 60 mpg. Elapsed time for the

The 1985 XLH had spoke wheels, chromed pipes, stepped seat and high bars. Harley-Davidson photo.

1962 was 14.2 sec., the 1984 did the quarter mile in 13.88 sec. Magazines didn't dare test brakes in 1962, but in 1984 the XLX stopped from 60 mph in 112 ft. For comparison, *Road & Track* said the brakes on a BMW M635CSi were "absolutely splendid" because they stopped the car from 60 in 141 ft.

And so it goes. The 1985 and late 1984, with light clutch and alternator, are better than early 1984, the 1983 and the 1982 with stiff frames, which in turn . . . you get the idea. All the way back, this works.

This is also common knowledge, so Sportsters depreciate in a straight line; that is, the newer it is the more it will cost you, while the less you pay, the less you get.

Choice two, restoration, changes this some. By definition restoration implies a need to be restored, which one hopes won't be true for that low-mileage 1983 XLX.

Older examples are rare. The Sunday classifieds will often have a 1983 for perhaps $4,000 and a 1973 for $2,000. What you won't often find is a 1963 XLCH or XLH.

Throw in here the sad fact that Sportsters are often abused, just as Electra Glides are maintained and Super Glides are modified. The Sportster has been the cheapest (V-twin) Harley all its life. Secondhand ones tend to wind up in the clumsy hands of owners who won't take the trouble to keep them right, or who spend their money on extended forks or stroker kits.

Despite this (or because of it) prices for straight, stock, solid older examples are moving up, as in $3,500 asking price for a 1963 XLH: I don't know if he got it, but he wasn't going to sell for less so he probably did, or will.

Interchangeability of parts, so helpful when you're repairing or restoring, makes the older bikes tricky. Few will be as they came from the factory twenty-five years ago.

Check the numbers. There were no frame numbers until 1970. From 1957 through 1969, the engine numbers are on a pad on the left side, between the cylinders. They have the model year and type, as in 57XL, 63XLCH. Easy. From 1970 through 1980 the number is on the right crankcase half, in code: 3A is XLH, 4A is XLCH, 4E is XLS and 7F is XLCR. There's a letter for the decade; H is the seventies, J is 1980 and the last number is the year of that decade; H8 is 1978.

You might want to check the year first because from 1981 through 1986 there's still another system. There are letters for the model: CA is XLH, CB is XLS, CC is XLX and CD is XR-1000. Next comes a letter for engine size; the Sportster is 61 cu. in. or H, the big twins are 80 cu. in. or K. There will be a digit, 1, for the regular model year; or if it's a mid-year, it will have a 2. Then there are model letters for year; B is 1981, C is 1982, D is 1983, E is 1984 and F is 1985.

Save these notes. I didn't understand them until I went to look at engines, then referred back to the codes.

The Sportster's weak points were built in, so to speak. The drum brakes were more reliable than effective. The frames and forks on the early machines flexed. Generators wore early and often. Until 1982 they all used oil, and leaked oil unless you took extra care and plenty of sealer and gasket cement and silicone.

All XL engines sounded terrible. They clanked and rattled and vibrated. Although the normal rules applied, an engine could be sound, have compression, not pump oil and still make what could be terminal noise. All you can do is inspect and test and hope.

Parts are a jungle. The demand isn't as strong for Sportsters as it is for the big twins. A complete swap list is impossible here, but for instance, you can use the same rocker box and pushrod tube gaskets for all XL engines, 1957 through 1985, and either one of two

Year and model	1983 XLX (Sportster)
Engine	ohv 45° V-twin
Bore and stroke	3.188x3.812 in.
Displacement	61 cu. in.
BHP	n/a
Gearbox	4 speeds
Shift	left foot
Wheelbase	60 in.
Wheels	19F/16R
Suspension	telescopic forks, swing-arm rear
Weight	468 lb. (dry)
Seat height	29 in.
MPG	60
Top speed	108 mph

primary cover gaskets. On the other hand, there were three different seals used for the magneto mount. The factory made the fiberglass fender and seat for just two years, yet at the first swap meet I came to, I found three of them, $25 each. What I had trouble finding are the little keepers for the screws on the clutch cover, as used on all Sportsters 1957-69. Why, I don't know.

Rule here is, everything is out there; be prepared to search and to become an expert.

Most of this becomes a benefit when we get to Choice three, building your personal best. You can put a magneto or high pipes on an XLH, convert your CH to points in the cover, install a 1000 cc engine in an 883 frame, put a kick start in your XR-1000, bolt your 900 engine into an XR frame and add TT-style Ceriani forks and dual disc brakes, or put a single-plane dual seat on an XLT or an XLT tank on your dual-seat XLH. . . . Once more, the list is limited only by your budget or your imagination.

Rating: Impossible

Now, wait. The rating system can work here, but it's a tight fit.

First is the late-breaking news. Just as this research was finished, Harley-Davidson announced a new Sportster, improved almost beyond description and at a price that, while it will bring in swarms of buyers, will also knock some numbers off all the Sportsters that preceded it.

But don't turn the page just yet. Unless you already own a Sporty, you haven't lost a dime. You may in fact gain when the owners lose.

Back to the three-tier system of buying a Sportster. For the first option, looking for a good machine to ride, all the used Sportsters are three stars. Decide how much you can

And the 1985 XLS had cast wheels, lower bars, stepped seat and large fuel tank with console. Any of the components could be used on any of the models, which was how the factory got three models from the same pieces. For fun, flip back to the pictures of the first Sportster and the first Model K and see how much things have changed and how much they remain the same. Harley-Davidson photo.

spend and get the best bike in that price range, the newer the better.

For the third path, your very own version of what the factory should have done, most of the above applies: You'll need to decide which stock Sportster comes the closest, then work toward the improvements. It would be more practical to backdate an XLX, with a larger tank and better seat, than to buy a 1961 XLH and install electric start and disc brakes.

But that may not matter. If you want a certain machine, that's the one to have and devil take investment potential.

Romance taken care of, ratings in terms of potential value for special editions are as follows.

As noted during the course of the Sportster's history, there have been several limited edition models. They don't quite fit the pattern but deserve separate mention.

Four stars: XLCH with fiberglass rear fender and seatbase, 1970

This model didn't sell well, and there aren't many of them. But because of that, and because they look different while using stock mechanical components and because you can find the few different bits if they aren't there, this model should—well, make that could—have extra value in years to come.

Evolution indeed. The new-for-1986 Sportster XLH-883 was a much revised version of the previous iron-barrel XL-1000 but the rest of the bike was XLX-61: solo seat, peanut tank, same suspension and brakes, diaphragm clutch spring and oil filler at the front of the cases where the generator was and an alternator inside the primary case. The primary case cover was supposed to look like those on the XR-750, although it doesn't to this XR-750 owner. Harley-Davidson photo.

Three stars: Anniversary models

These include the 1973, celebrating Harley's seventieth; the 1976, celebrating America's Bicentennial; and the 1978, celebrating the Sportster's twenty-fifth.

They were made to be collected and they have nothing exceptional except for the decals and labels and paint. Good bikes but not worth extra now, nor in future, unless the buyer is just crazy for decals.

Three stars: XLCR, 1977-78

This is a tough one. I like the CR. It's got a bigger tank and better seat than the mass-produced Sportsters during these model years. It's faster and I like its looks.

However. People began talking collector item even before the XLCR proved a sales flop. This led owners to expect extra money. I've seen ads with high asking prices while a friend who tried to sell his didn't get Nibble One. Seeing as how there's an even closer race replica now, I can't see this one as an investment.

Four stars: XR-1000, 1983-85

Right, the XR-1000 didn't sell when brand new and there may still be new ones on the floor. But I think the price held sales down—that and the lack of visibility.

Plus, the XR-1000 really is a racer. Stock ones routinely win in the AMA's Battle of the Big Twins class. Modified XR-1000s win their class in the series. And a highly modified version, actually more like an XR-750 in road race trim but with a 1000 cc engine, has won the BOTT at Daytona three years running, even when the Ducatis have national or world champion riders.

Better still, people are right now discounting these bikes. The factory probably won't ever make a machine like this again; they're rare enough to be collected and numerous enough to be collected (follow that?). The public was wrong on this one.

Four stars: Kick-start 883, 1957-67

Early Sportsters are more of a risk, because they're hard to find in good shape, and expensive to restore. But they do look different and they do offer something, as in skill: Notice that in *Then Came Bronson* he rides a Sporty with electric start but he always kicks it because that's what real bikers do. If collecting motorcycles continues to grow as a hobby, the early Sportsters will be fertile ground, sort of like the early Chevy V-8s when all the Corvettes had been priced out of the average market.

Three stars: Electric start and 1000, 1968-85

Yes, these are better machines, more likely to be in good condition when found, equipped with better brakes and so forth. But there are lots of them and they lack, to me at least, the good looks of the early ones and the better mechanicals of the newest. Just because a nice one can be a bargain doesn't mean it's a good investment.

Evolution Sportster

Predictable needn't mean dull. All through the history of Harley's V-Twins there runs a pattern: H-D revises the engine, then puts it into a proven chassis, followed later by a revised chassis for the now-proven engine.

That's just what we had here, with the new-for-1986 Evolution Sportster. The new part was the Evolution part. Viewed overall, the 1986 Sportster engine—there were two versions of the same engine but we'll get to that—was obviously based on the earlier XLs, but incorporating lessons learned from the V2 (1340) FL and the XR750 (racing) engines.

The V2XL (my initials, not the factory's) was much newer than it looked. In effect, it was the same engine in two displacements. The first one shown was the XLH-883. As that number hinted, it displaced 883 cc (same size as that first XL from 1957), and it had the original bore and stroke of 3.00 x 3.812 in.

Six weeks after Harley unveiled the 883, it brought out another Sportster, the XLH-1100. This was the same engine except that the bore was 3.35 in. and the displacement 1100 cc. The different bore meant different pistons and larger valves but all other engine parts of the 883 and the 1100 were the same.

The V2XL had alloy barrels with iron liners, like the XR and the V2FL. The alloy heads had two valves per cylinder, set at a narrow angle. The pentroof head and flat-topped piston formed an efficient combustion chamber that allowed a compression ratio of 9:1 and a recommendation of unleaded fuel. The rocker boxes were in layers, so they and the heads and barrels could come off with the engine in the frame. They looked like the tiered rocker boxes on the V2FL, and while the pieces wouldn't interchange, the assemblies would.

The V2XL had hydraulic valve lifters, like the larger Harley twin, and the flywheels were forged in one piece, that is, the mainshafts were part of the flywheels instead of being pressed into them. (Forged one-piece flywheels have been used in the XR engines since 1971.)

The new engine used the diaphragm spring clutch and alternator from the later, older engines, post mid-1984. The factory calculated that the earlier, iron XL engines had 455 parts, including fasteners. The new XL had 426 parts (29 fewer), and 206 of the 426 were new.

The cases, primary cover and timing cover were new and didn't interchange. The new engine used the same rear engine mount but a different front mount and the frame's top tube was revised to accommodate the different heads and rocker boxes. Thus, the alloy XR engine wouldn't swap with the iron versions.

Back on familiar territory, the new engine came in a familiar package; what amounts to the XLX frame and equipment.

The catalog listed two 1986 Sportsters. Both used the initials XLH; no more C or CH

The XLH-1100 had exactly the same frame and suspension as the XLH-883, but got a larger bore, larger valves, more displacement and 10 more horses (63 instead of 53). The 1100 had a stepped seat, passenger pegs, higher bars and more choices of trim and colors. And the price was $1,200 higher. The parts interchanged, that is, the larger seat fit the 883, the lower bars went on the 1100. The two versions of the new engine and XLX cycle parts were the entire 1986 Sportster line-up. Harley-Davidson photo.

or X or S or T. The designations were thus XLH-883 and XLH-1100.

The 883 was the price leader, supposed to attract the budget-minded buyer or (more likely) the person who'd like a Harley but didn't want to pay more than Japanese prices.

Year and model	1986 XLH-883
Engine	ohv 45° V-twin
Bore and stroke	3.00x3.81 in.
Displacement	54 cu. in.
BHP	42 (net)
Gearbox	4 speeds
Shift	left foot
Wheelbase	60 in.
Wheels	19F/16R
Suspension	telescopic forks, swing-arm rear
Weight	478 lb. (curb)
Seat height	30 in.
MPG	54
Top speed	113 mph (calculated)

Suggested retail for the 883 was an astonishing $3,995. Yes, $3,995. For that you got a solo seat, speedometer and low bars.

The 1100 listed for $5,199 and came with tach and speedo, a stepped dual seat, passenger pegs, pullback bars and more choices of color—two-tone and candy on up to the Liberty Edition with decals endorsing the restoration of the Statue of Liberty.

The Evolution Sportster was a calculated gamble. The 883 was a loss leader, intended to get people to buy Harley or at least come to the showroom. It was rated at 53 bhp and early tests show it was slower than the iron 1000 XLX and the Japanese V-twins. The 1100 sold for $1,200 more than the 883, and $2,000

The Evolution Sportster was announced late in 1985, as an early 1986 model. Basically it was an all-alloy version of the XL engine, displacing either 883 or 1100 cc, in the existing XLX chassis. Harley-Davidson photo.

less than the next Harley in line, the basic FXR. The 1100 was rated at 63 bhp and thus moved the alloy XL into the same neighborhood as the iron 1000 Sportsters or rival Honda 1100s.

Using one frame and suspension and two versions of the same drivetrain, Harley-Davidson set out to build a line of models named Sportster.

Model Year 1987

It's worth saying here that the XL package has always been mix and match. From the first day of the Evo XLs, the buyer was provided a solo seat, black paint, low bars and peanut tank, with the option of dual

XLH-883 had a suggested retail price of $3,995. It came with a small tank, low bars and speedometer but no tach; pretty much the new, smaller engine in the XLX package. For the base price, you got a choice of black or red; for another $75 you could have candy red or candy blue. Harley-Davidson photo.

The evolved Sportster engine was much newer than it looked. The cases were changed for a new front engine mount, while the barrels and cylinder heads were aluminum. The 883 engine had a three-inch bore while the 1100 version had a bore of 3.35 in. Both had the same 3.8125 in. stroke as the iron 1000 cc XL engine, which had been discontinued. The cylinders' included angle was still 45° and the two-valve heads were nearly identical to the earlier V2 big twin engine. Harley-Davidson photo.

The designers were careful to keep the alloy XL engine as much like the iron XL as they could. But the front engine mount was changed and the new engine couldn't bolt into earlier frames, unlike the previous versions. The spin-on oil filter was where the generator used to be and the generator was replaced by an alternator, inside the primary case behind the diaphragm spring clutch. The factory said it couldn't cram any more gears into the gearbox cavity, so the 883 (shown) and 1100 (with contrasting blackened fins) versions of the alloy engine still had four forward speeds. Harley-Davidson photo.

seat, paint schemes, buckhorn bars and within a year of the model's introduction, a king peanut tank, same shape but higher and holding 3.25 gal.

The 1987 model year saw the introduction of a semi-new model, the Hugger. What it hugged was the ground, as the rear shock mounts were moved back and the shocks tilted, for a lower static height with the same wheel travel. The seat was given different material for the padding.

Read this carefully. What the press releases never said was that the Hugger was designed for short people, read here women.

This must have been a touchy issue. Women have always been part of motorcycling, ever since daring young ladies in 1911 rode cross-country, honest. But women have always been a small percentage of the biking public and every twenty years, make that every generation, there's the notion that girls have just now become brave enough to ride astride.

Nonsense. Bravado may be a masculine trait, but bravery knows no gender.

Nor was H-D reluctant to attract their share of women customers. Equally factual, women are on average shorter than men and all riders like having their boots reach the ground at stoplights, while also equally, the women who wanted motorcycles didn't want girls' bikes.

So first, the Hugger was advertised as having a static seat height of 26.75 in., 1.75 in. lower than the stock XLs. Second, when you read the fine print you were told some of this came from compressing the seat material and that the compression was measured by using a rider with a dressed weight of 185 lb.

Not your average sweet young thing, in other words. Bit shakey in the true facts department. But never mind, the Hugger surely got some new people into the sport, and that's no bad thing.

Elsewhere in the model year, the XLs got some revisions of the internal ratios in the gearbox, with first, second and third all taller; mostly this put third closer to top gear, so you buzzed the engine less passing on the highway.

The cylinder heads got new combustion chambers, modelled after the XR-750 racer's design, and the 1100 heads were reworked, with smaller ports and valves, which increased the velocity of the charge and improved efficiency. The mods were worth five percent more power, the factory said.

Model Year 1988

Time for the other shoe. Turned out the 1100 had been for practice. In 1988, the larger of the small twins got bored out again, from 3.35 to 3.50 in., taking the displacement to a full 1200 cc, or 74 ci. Yes, same as the old F series big twins, although the original 74s had smaller bores and longer strokes and Harley-Davidson has always called the XL 1200 just that, not the 74.

This was as good and timely a move as H-D could have made. With one stroke, as the Irish might put it, the big-bore Sportster was back in the performance park.

We'll compare different years and even publications here, but the tests from *Cycle* and *Cycle World* show:

Model	Weight	Quarter Mile	0-60 mph
1991 XL1200	494 lb.	13.00 sec.	4.0 sec.
1987 XL1100	475 lb.	13.15 sec.	Not given
1988 XL883	478 lb.	14.24 sec.	4.96 sec.

A flat 13 sec. quarter mile sees off every production car on the market, and keeps pace with the rival big twins from the other makers and perhaps best of all, the XL1200 will out-drag the FXRS, skill and conditions being equal.

Why does this matter most? Because the Big Twin crowd has always mocked the XLs, with terms like Baby Bike, Girl's Bike and even—this from Arlen Ness—Paperboy Bike. Ouch. And nyah nyah to them, because the 1200 returns us Sportster fans to those thrilling days of yesteryear, when the XLCH was Bad and the FLH was merely Big. About time, too.

Model Years 1989–90

Two years at once because the XLH line was undergoing a series of gradual steps, as the same components were moved about to create the impression of variety.

The basic XLH 883 had the solo seat, small tank, cast wheels and a speedometer as the only instrument. The Deluxe XLH had a dual seat with passenger pegs, laced wheels and a choice of paint colors, as in red or blue. The Hugger had solo seat and cast wheels but was lower, as mentioned, and there were buckhorn bars to put the controls closer to the rider. With the XLH 1200 you got most of the extras, with two-tone paint, tach and speedo, buckhorn bars and dual seat.

Thus, the dealer could offer more choice than a list of options. Better throw in here that there were the options and the trades, so don't be surprised to see an Evo XL with low bars, laced wheels, dual saddle and tach only. The Sportster has always been the most adaptable of Harleys.

Model Year 1991

Gradual change was eclipsed in 1991 by two big jumps: First, the venerable four-speed gearbox became a five speed.

This took lots of engineering time and talent and resulted in a new clutch and shift mechanism. The ratios were juggled so top gear, the final drive ratio, was taller than before and first, as in crawling around crowded parking lots, was lower and the gap from first to second, second to third, and on up, was less. It took more than putting five pairs of gears where four had been. The result was a more pleasant motorcycle with only half an inch of width added to the package.

Second, the 1200 and the 883 Deluxe got belt final drive.

This was just as logical and surely less work. H-D and suppliers began this one ten years earlier on some of the big twins—see other chapters for details—and the belt has proven itself as tough and durable and quiet and less mess. For price and marketing reasons, the two top XLs got belts and the

Moving up the Sportster line, we find the 883 Deluxe. It'll have the dual seat, dual instruments, lace-up wheels and paint other than basic black. Depending on year, it will come with either chain or belt final drive. Harley-Davidson photo.

HARLEY-DAVIDSON
SPORTSTER
EVOLUTION

cheaper two kept chain, while for ease of manufacture, all the Sportsters from 1991 on have been five speeds forward.

And as still another extension of choice, the factory offered a kit, by which the chain drive of older XLs can be replaced with belt.

Model Year 1992

More consolidation here, as the only major change for the XLH line was another rework of the suspension and seat for the Hugger. That dropped static height another 1.5 in., 3 in. lower than the XLH plain, and earned the title Super Hugger.

Beyond that, the two chain-drive models got o-ring chains, and all the XLs received different brake pad material and such.

What to look for

Stretching the rules here, and admitting that the XL line is the budget line, the entry-level for Harley-Davidson, we'll include some ideas on how to buy a *new* Sportster: Pick and choose.

I say this because the price structure at H-D can leave something for the consumer to desire. The 1992 price list, for instance, began at $4499 for the XLH plain, $5075 for the Super Hugger, $5559 for the Deluxe and $6400 for the 1200. You'll pay a couple hundred for other than black paint on the basic version, same for a big tank new from the factory, and the same goes for a better seat or pipes.

This is called pick and choose because if you have some desires and some knowledge of what you want, you can meet and beat the factory. Last time I looked, I got a used 3.5 gal. Superglide tank for $100, in good shape. You can unbolt the fenders and tank and negotiate a paint job of your design and color for less than the factory's price, a seat from

Top model is the XLH 1200. It comes with cast wheels, dual seat, high bars and two-tone paint. Keep in mind that the dealer will be happy to fit high bars on the plain machine, low bars and black paint on the 1200 . . . and that you can do it yourself, for less. Harley-Davidson photo.

Corbin or Young works better than the H-D extra version, ditto for exhaust systems.

In strictly technical terms, I can't imagine any rider who's been through a blow-out with laced wheels and tubes, and a deflation with cast wheels and tubeless tires, who would not prefer cast wheels and tubeless. They are safer, period, and I don't give a hoot for Retro Style, not on this issue.

Further, the good ol' Motor Company has provided for us skinflints. You can buy a kit for the belt drive and new barrels and pistons to take your 883 to 1200 in the privacy of your own home, as the ads say.

My point? The XLH 883 is *the* bargain in today's market. If you can buy one new, fix the easy stuff like seat and tank and paint, then wear out the stock chain and top end and upgrade as maintenance and you've got a personalized Sporty that'll run with the FXRs.

What to look for, used.

This is shameless, but when the Evo XL came out, I, your resident expert, fearlessly predicted it would be good from Day One.

I was pret' near right. There was a recall for flaws in the cast wheels, and for some shifting bothers. My own XL locked in gear with the very flaw the factory warned me about. There were cases of mis-assembly of the relief valve in the oil pump and some leakage around the lifters in the timing case. At least one XL came through with not quite enough wire in the loom, that is, the taut wire snapped, but the kid and I fixed it at the side of the road. In brief, the Evo XL has done at least as well as any new H-D ever.

So first, the Evo models are better machines than the iron XLs. This has kept the price of used Evo examples up and pushed the older bikes down the scale.

Next, the plain 883 sells for less than a Deluxe or 1100, the five speed is preferred to the four speed, the belt to the chain and so on, as any free market student would expect. The best protection here is that you can so easily improve the 883 into a 1200 with belt drive that the bikes that came new with the improvements aren't quite as valuable as they'd be if you couldn't get the kits.

Rating: Three stars with cluster

Yeah, this is said over and over, but the fact is, the Evo Sportster has done well by doing good. It's the intro model, the best seller, trouble-free and priced to match the imports.

This is perfectly splendid for those of us who own 'em. It's good in the long run for those who will buy one and keep it to ride and enjoy. But because the XL's value is so clearly established, you aren't going to sneak up on an owner and scoop up a bargain for later sale. Nothing is hidden, everything is linear and analog.

If you aren't going to get rich, is what I'm saying here, neither can you go wrong.

Chapter 5

Singles and Imports

★★★	Hummers 1947-59
★★★	? Ranger, Pacer, Scat, Bobcat 1962-66
★	Rapidos etc. 1966-72
★★★★	Aermacchi Sprints 1961-74
★★★	Other Aermacchis
★	Aermacchi two-strokes 1973-77

When Harley-Davidson got into rough water several years ago the critics were ready. Harley's mistake, they said, was to stick with those dumb old V-twins instead of expanding the product line.

Wrong on two counts. First, Indian didn't stick with its big V-twins. When the English began to sell in the United States after World War II, Indian came out with smaller vertical twins in the English mode. The engines weren't very good; the money invested went down the drain and so did Indian.

When the Japanese went worldwide, BSA, Triumph and Norton put their research time and money into smaller engines with electric start, like the Japanese engines. The engines weren't very good; the money invested went down the drain and so did the English motorcycle industry.

Second, Harley didn't merely soldier on with the old-style V-twin. Harley's management people realized they needed different models. They tried for thirty years to make them and to interest people in them. If their smaller models didn't sell and their expansion program didn't work, well, they tried. And they made some pretty neat little bikes.

Hummers, 1947-59

As World War II drew to a close, anybody who bothered to look around could tell the postwar world would be different. And busy, as millions of people went after the material goods denied them by the war and the depression before that.

Harley-Davidson had big V-twins and medium V-twins, period. America was starved for transportation and there were young people who might be persuaded to travel astride while saving for a big bike (or a car, for shame).

Meanwhile, the Germans owed the Allies giant war debts, meaning the Allies could help themselves to anything they liked; for example, the design of a small motorcycle engine. This is just what Harley, in the United States, and BSA, in England, did. Both got the rights to DKW's design for a 125 cc two-stroke single, revised it for their own markets and went into the beginner motorcycle business.

There's some confusion here. The literature of the day says Harley's 125, introduced in 1947, was called the M-125. Harley's own history book says it was the S-125. The certified history says the Hummer name didn't come into use until the later-generation machines in 1955, while I have seen with my own eyes a stock 1953 model with "Hummer" cast into the top clamp. Somebody's records are wrong. I don't know whose, but because the name is useful I'm going to call them all Hummers.

Historical perspective: The modern two-stroke is an impressive device, more powerful for its weight and displacement than a four-stroke. Two-strokes rule racing everywhere they're allowed to compete.

It wasn't always so. Until the East Germans (getting even for the loss of that engine?) discovered how to make two-strokes work, and until engineer/rider Ernst Degner escaped from behind the Iron Curtain and gave Suzuki the inside scoop, the two-stroke was less powerful than the four-stroke and was useful only because the two-stroke had fewer moving parts and weighed less.

Thus, the new Harley 125 wasn't fast, nor was it supposed to be. The engine developed about 3 bhp. The bike had a 50 in. wheelbase, weighed maybe 200 lb. and had seating for one; sensible in that the one rider, flat on the tank with feet pointed straight out behind, might get the bike up to 55 mph.

It was a contemporary motorcycle, with foot shift and hand clutch. Rear suspension was rigid and the front used girder forks. This design had the entire assembly (wheel, hub and legs) pivoting up and down on the steering head; it wasn't like the leading link forks used on the big Harleys at the time.

In 1951, two years after the same thing was done for the big twin, the Hummer got telescopic forks and became the Tele-Glide.

The 125 cc two-stroke single was very different. Notice that back then not even factory publicity shots needed helmets, that women were encouraged to ride long before Gloria Steinem came along, and that windshields and saddlebags were offered for even the small machines. Harley-Davidson photo.

In 1953 the engine was enlarged to 165 cc and became the M-165 (or the S-165, depending on where you read it). Sales were encouraging and the factory brought back the 125 Hummer along with the S-165 from 1954 until 1959.

What to look for

You shouldn't have to look far. There were close to 100,000 two-stroke singles made and sold during this period. How many are left, nobody knows. But they're still turning up in dusty barns.

The bike almost certainly won't be purely stock. There were optional chrome-plated wheel rims and handlebars, and nearly all the runners will have a different tank or air cleaner or something. I've even seen a former rigid with a swing arm rear suspension, a kit offered by a New Jersey dealer. The cleaner the better is the only rule here.

Some parts, the ignition points and voltage regulators, for example, were shared with the big twins. Other bits aren't impossible to find, thanks to the specialty stores. You

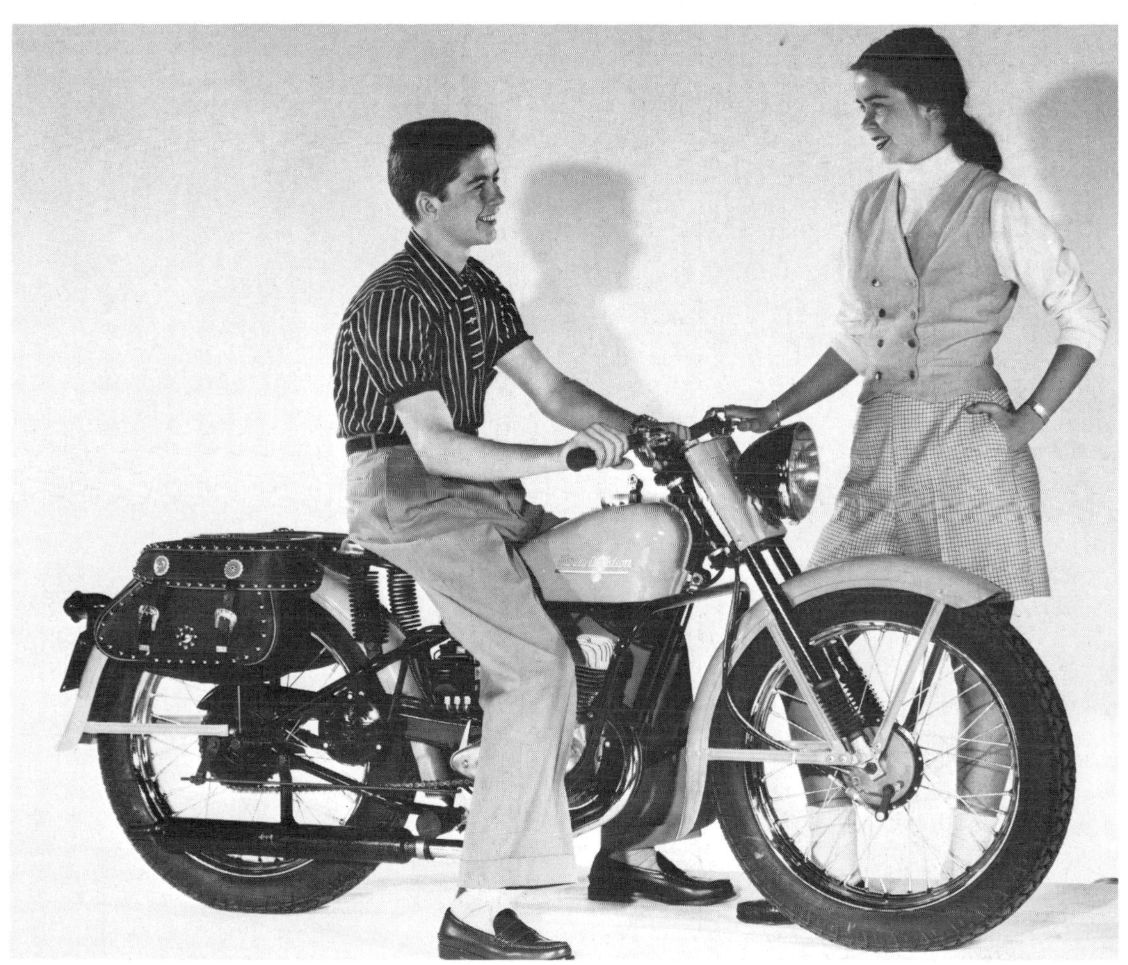

The M-165 had a larger version of the DKW-derived engine, telescopic forks and a fancier cover for the top clamps and headlight mount. Harley-Davidson photo.

may not be able to get the exact part needed for your model year but nobody seems to care much because nobody knows what really went where, when.

Rating: Three stars

No hurt feelings, okay? The Hummers were cute little rascals so there are people who love them. They appear in shows, all restored and sparkling.

However. They weren't distinguished machines when new. They were fine in town, getting to work or school and so forth, but they won't keep up with highway traffic and the little drum brakes won't stop in today's traffic. They weren't exotic and they weren't expensive so they seldom win show awards.

They aren't going to become valuable, in other words. They can be fun play riding in sheltered conditions and they're cheap to buy, restore and maintain. Not a bad hobby but not a good investment, either.

Year and model	1947 M-125 (aka S-125)
Engine	two-stroke single
Bore and stroke	2.06x2.28 in.
Displacement	7.6 cu. in.
BHP	3
Gearbox	3 speeds
Shift	right foot
Wheelbase	50 in.
Wheels	19 in.
Suspension	girder forks, rigid rear
Weight	200 lb. (est.)
Seat height	n/a
MPG	n/a
Top speed	55 mph (est.)

Ranger, Pacer, Scat and Bobcat, 1962-66

Harley did a fairly good business in the lightweights, all things considered. The English did better, but both suffered when the Japanese got busy in the early sixties.

H-D management people could see the wave of the future coming, so before it swamped them, they had a large number of different products. There were scooters and

Girder forks on the first 125 gave way to telescopic forks, and the name became Tele-Glide. It still had the rigid rear end, though. Harley-Davidson photo.

mopeds and tinybikes (none of which will be discussed here as they weren't really motorcycles). There were Italian-made motorcycles. H-D bought Aermacchi, a fine old firm fallen on hard times of its own. (We know this now as "moving offshore," American companies finding cheaper places to get hired help.)

And there were homebuilt two-strokes, made in profusion while Harley was bringing in the Aermacchi two-strokes and four-strokes, as will be detailed later.

The 1960 and 1961 offering was called the Super 10; pretty much the Hummer 165 but with the engine souped to 9 bhp, or restricted to 5 bhp in states where fourteen-year-olds were allowed to ride little motorcycles. (Guess how long it took us to remove the restrictors.) In case your state was one of these innocent places, the label was BT for the powerful one, BTU for the other.

The domestic names and models expanded in 1962, with the Ranger, Pacer and Scat. The Ranger was strictly dirt, with 165 cc engine, 18 in. wheels and no lights. The Pacer was road only, with low fenders and exhaust pipe. The Scat had high fenders, high pipe and lights. Pacer and Scat both had 175 cc, while all three used telescopic forks and rigid rear.

Italian design appeared on the domestic models in 1963. The Ranger was dropped while Pacer and Scat got an unusual rear suspension: The springs were beneath the engine. This was done by several Italian makers, Moto Guzzi for one and Aermacchi for another.

Leaf back in this book to the Super Glide section and look at the FXST. Wow! Springs beneath the engine. When Harley brought out this design in 1984 the company was proud. Rightfully so, as it works and it sells. But nobody seemed to remember it had done it twenty years earlier.

Anyway, the design was good work. The dirt-bike boom didn't begin until after Bruce Brown's movie, *On Any Sunday*, and after the arrival of Yamaha's DT-1, a 250 cc dual-purpose bike that made off-road fun easy to get to.

The 1959 Hummer was a basic machine, what with its sprung solo saddle, solid rear suspension, bulb horn and no mirror. But it provided transportation and fun, and while the market lasted, the little two-strokes were profitable. They're not suited to life in today's fast lane but they can be inexpensively bought and restored at home. Harley-Davidson photo.

Surprise. The Scat had rear suspension, in the form of a swing arm controlled by spring/shocks under the engine, not unlike the current Softail.

But the Scat was a good trail bike, used to get into the back country for fishing and exploring. Armando Magri used to replace the Scat's 20:1 first gear with the 30:1 gear from the old 125s, giving more engine power at lower road (or trail) speeds. It could climb out of anything that way. Magri promoted the models and had about 300 customers running through the California mountains back then. Never had to tow one home, he says.

The Scat and Pacer were joined in 1965-66 by a model with a fiberglass rear fender/seat base/tank cover. You could get a full dual seat or a shorter seat with a luggage rack on the back. Odd looking, I think now and don't recall ever seeing one.

I must not be the only one. For every dealer like Magri, who was willing to develop the market, there were scores who didn't know and didn't want to know. Harley couldn't sell enough at made-here prices so they were dropped.

What to look for

At a glance the 1965 Scat looks just like the 1955 Hummer. The basic difference is the rear suspension, so everything said about the Hummer applies to the Scat, Pacer and Bobcat except perhaps they'd be more comfortable.

Rating: Three charitable stars

I could be wrong about this. I never expected 1954 Chevrolets to become trendy. But unless you fall hopelessly in love, stay clear. If you bought one tomorrow what you'd have would be a used motorcycle without much power and with less chance of becoming a classic in the future.

Rapidos and their siblings, 1966-72

Italy was of course a much better place to sell small motorcycles, so Aermacchi already had a selection ready for export. Harley began bringing in 50 cc machines, really more like motorized bicycles and useful only

By 1965 the Scat looked dated—a lot like the earlier Hummer. The two levers on the left side of the engine cases weren't a rocker shift, by the way. The low one was the shift lever, the high one was the kick-start lever.

in cities or at the beach. The engines were enlarged to 65 cc, still no takers. They were finally pushed out the dealership doors through heavy discounting.

The lesson here seemed clear enough, so in 1968 Harley imported a larger model, coded M-125 and named Rapido. It had a 125 cc two-stroke single-cylinder engine, with nothing except size and type in common with the earlier 125, and a four-speed gearbox. The parts were perfectly normal—telescopic forks, dual rear shocks, hand clutch and foot shift.

The Rapido began as a street bike, then became the M-125 street version and the ML-125 street/trail in 1969. The street model was dropped in 1970 while the scrambler continued through 1972.

Meanwhile, the basic model was stripped of excess parts and sleeved down to 100 cc in 1970. It was named the Baja 100 (after the point-to-point race in Baja, California). The Baja 100 was a souped-up little speedster with ported cylinder, 11.5:1 compression ratio, expansion chamber and five-speed gearbox with choice of wide or close ratios. The Rapido 125 had 10 bhp while the Baja 100 had about 12. It won some races. Indeed, surely it was built for the 100 cc class in desert races and enduros. It, too, was built through 1972.

What to look for

In one word, don't. While the Rapido and Baja were acceptable motorcycles for their purpose in their time, they've been seriously outmoded. Nor are they historic,

The Bobcat was an experiment in style; the domestic two-stroke engine, frame and suspension were shared with the Scat, but the Bobcat had a fiberglass fender, seat base and tank cover. Ahead of its time, one might say. Harley-Davidson photo.

nor is anybody collecting them. If you need a runabout and find one real cheap, okay, risk the $100. As projects for restoration, hobby racing, shows, even labors of love, they just aren't worth it.

Note here the lack of mention of the smaller Italians with the Harley label, the M65 Sports, X-90s and so forth offered for sale (but not sold often enough) during this period. There are motorcycles that did their job in the past and should be allowed to fade away—and these are some of them.

Aermacchi Sprints, 1961-74

Now we get back to the good stuff. Europeans were as ready for change and prosperity after World War II as Americans were, but they didn't have the natural resources and it took them longer. So they supported moped, noped and scooter companies until they could afford minicars and then real cars. (Americans did the same thing, but it was after World War I.)

What this meant was that Aermacchi had an excellent line of real motorcycles ready when Harley needed them. They were powered by 250 cc four-stroke singles, had suspension at both ends and controls in conventional places. They used backbone frames, a large central tube from steering head to swing arm pivot, with the engine suspended below the tube. Like several other Italian makers, Aermacchi used a horizontal cylinder projecting forward from the crank-

The Italian-made Rapido, shown in 1968 version, was a 125 cc two-stroke that shared only type and size with the domestic singles. The Rapido was obviously European, and was as speedy as it looked. Harley-Davidson photo.

case/gearbox, keeping the center of gravity low and leaving room for the carburetor, airbox and battery.

The first Aermacchi four-strokes were imported in 1961. They were full road bikes with what now looks like lots of bodywork. When motorcycles were transportation, the makers provided full fenders that shielded the rider from mud and water, a practice mostly abandoned in the sport bike era, alas.

The first model was coded C and named Sprint. To us now, it may look like a Japanese motorcycle from the past, but that's mostly because back then the Japanese patterned their style on Italian machines. They later used the English look and now they're replica Harleys but that, too, is another story.

The Sprint C sold well, and in 1962 it was joined by the H (old Harley lettering dies hard). The H was the sports bike, a scrambler

The Sprint H (a 1962 model here) was the sports bike, with low seat, really nice tank and high fenders and exhaust pipe. *Cycle World* photo.

with skimpy fenders, smaller tank and seat. There was also an option, the Sprint R, with no lights, a higher compression ratio, exhaust megaphone and tachometer.

Baby Sportsters is what the Sprint C and Sprint H were. *Cycle World* tested a Sprint H in 1962. It hit 76 in half a mile, did the standing quarter mile in 19.2 sec. and went 0-60 in 15 sec. With the 2.6 gal. fuel tank full, it weighed 280 lb.

Car Life tested a Sprint C the same year. It got a top speed of 72.5 mph, a 19.5 sec. quarter mile and 0-60 in 16.8 sec. The listed weight was 275 lb. *Cycle World* estimated power at 21 bhp, *Car Life* guessed 18.

Odd. The engines were supposed to be the same. The C used more parts and had a 4 gal. tank and 17 in. wheels. The H had a 2.6 gal. tank, 18 in. wheels and longer forks and shocks. The H should have been faster, which it was, but it should also have been lighter, which it wasn't.

Well. The Sprint H was renamed the Scrambler in 1964 and got a bigger carburetor, higher compression ratio, tuned exhaust and 25 bhp.

All the 1967 250s had a new version of the engine, with alloy head and barrel, shorter stroke and larger bore. The Sprint SS, a scrambler with lower case s, got more ground clearance and detachable headlight; and the Sprint H got a cleaner fuel tank. The clubman racer model was the CRS, an SS stripped of road-legal parts.

This was a tough market. Yamaha had the DT-1, the neat little two-stroke single. Honda had the SL-350, a twin with off-road looks if not motocross capability. The sporting two-strokes were on the rise and Honda's four-strokes used overhead cams while the Harleys still had humble pushrods.

Year and model	1962 Sprint C
Engine	ohv single
Bore and stroke	2.60x2.84 in.
Displacement	15 cu. in.
BHP	18 (claimed)
Gearbox	4 speeds
Shift	right foot
Wheelbase	52 in.
Wheels	17 in.
Suspension	telescopic forks, swing-arm rear
Weight	275 lb. (curb)
Seat height	n/a
MPG	50
Top speed	75 mph

So in 1969 Harley-Aermacchi gave the engine a longer stroke, for a displacement of 350 cc. The models were SS-350, the SS standing for Street Scrambler, and ERS, dirt only.

Cycle World's SS-350 weighed 323 lb. at the curb, hit 92 mph, did the quarter mile in 15.85 sec., got to 60 mph in 8 sec. and returned 46 mpg. It was much faster and thus more powerful than the 250. Before your test ride, though, note that the kick lever was on the left and the right-side shift was one up, three down, the opposite of the domestic pattern.

Still hoping to attract customers, Harley gave the SS-350 and SX-350 (street only, with the low fenders) electric start in 1973. It didn't help; well, it might have helped people who had trouble with kick start, but sales didn't pick up and the four-stroke Aermacchis were dropped after the 1974 model year.

What to look for

Sprints tend to be found in one of two conditions. One, they were bought new by somebody who didn't ride much, so they're nice and clean. Or two, they went through a series of desperate or unhappy owners so they're rats, bangers, barely operable.

These machines were better than their reputation. They were solid, in a general way, but they fell victim to a kind of culture shock.

In Italy a 250 or 350 was an adult motorcycle, priced and designed for the mature, responsible rider. The engine was small because of tax structure. Sprints were built for people who took care of their bikes.

But in America a 250 was a toy, a kiddybike. This more prosperous society considered Sprints as something for the youngsters to thrash around on. As all parents know, the average kid can break an anvil with a rubber hammer. Sprints were used, abused and put away wet.

Further, Italian and English motorcycles had two things in common: They both had two wheels and they both had weak electrical systems. Why, I don't know. I suspect it's because both countries and their customers were isolated from the rest of the world until about ten years ago. They didn't know electrical components could be reliable. (Now, incidentally, some Italian motorcycles come with Japanese switchgear, just like Harleys do.)

Adding to that, Aermacchi made only the engines. All the rest was bought from outside suppliers. Italian subcontractors were sometimes great, sometimes terrible. Nor could the Harley home office get better service.

So what you look for is the normal stuff, as in rusted frames, bent tubes, engines that rattle or belch smoke. Then check the wiring loom. Either it will be stock but in a terrible tangle, or previous owners will have tried to patch it, leaving it in a terrible tangle. Be ready to yank it all off. Throw away everything except the lights, ignition and basic charging system, then replace with American bulbs and wire and Japanese connections and switches.

Rating: Four for the best

The redeeming feature here is that the Sprints are basically sound, once you manage to keep the ignition dry. And they're lovely, especially the later H models with that graceful tank. So any sound Sprint is worth three stars, a good buy for its use and what you'll get back when you sell.

Sprints are beginning to turn up in shows. Most of the parts can be found, albeit

The Sprint C had a larger fuel tank, thicker seat, covers for the shocks and fork tubes and fuller fenders. Engines and frames were the same for the two models. *Cycle World* photo.

you'll have to look for them. The engine always was competitive, in fact it still is in countries with classes for single-cylinder four-strokes.

The later, short-stroke 250 is better than the early version and the early 350 is less cluttered than the one with electric start.

In sum, a clean H model, 1967 or 1968, or an SS-350 or ERS, 1969 through 1972, can be bought for a good price, restored at home and used under any conditions. Perhaps the H models will gain in value as more people seek them out, which makes them rate four stars.

Other Aermacchis

Although Harley-Davidson had a controlling interest in Aermacchi during the sixties and early seventies, the Italian firm maintained its own operations at home and exported some models under its own name during that time.

When Harley's investment arrived, Aermacchi was building and exporting four versions of what was to become the Harley Sprint. These were the Ala Bianca (White Wing) and Ala Azzurra (Light Blue Wing), 175 and 250 cc all-purpose bikes; and the Ala Rossa (Red Wing) and Ala Verde (Green Wing), the same 175 and 250 cc engines but with higher compression ratio and lower handlebars. Odd though it sounds, the Red Wing was painted gray and the Green Wing was red and silver.

Harley's investment went for improved product. The Sprint, as sold in the US, was an improved version of the Ala Verde. The Italian version was named in tribute to Harley's home state, the "Wisconsin." No kidding.

The machines evolved at home just as they did in the US, becoming less adult transportation and more semi-sports. Outside the US the Sprint C, with large tank, was called the Ala Blu (Blue Wing) and the smaller-tank Sprint H was the Ala Verde.

Names went out of fashion about the time the 350 engine arrived. The American SS-350 was sold as the Sprint 350 in England and the GTS in Italy, where there was also a bigger-tank model called the GT.

What to look for

Small motorcycles had competition worldwide by this time. Aermacchi had other rivals in Italy and was faced with import duties and the Japanese in England, so while there were many models, there weren't all that many sales.

A few hundred four-stroke singles were sold in England, many more elsewhere. They are being restored, but the restorers say there are problems finding the exact part because no two bikes seem to have been alike.

Major mechanical parts are easier to find, as the racers are active. Try FLC Imports in England or inquire through Cagiva, the Italian motorcycle maker that's thriving under its own name and owns the name, rights and presumably the parts of Aermacchi that remain.

Rating: Three stars

Competition is a problem for the Aermacchi singles because Moto Guzzi and Ducati have more snob appeal at home, while a raft of English bikes have a home team advantage there and in the United States. But the Aermacchis are good bikes and there's been some renewed interest in recent years, so they now rate at least average, more if they strike your fancy.

Aermacchi two-strokes, 1973-77

The four-strokes were dropped because the two-strokes had taken over. They'd always been lighter and simpler, but now their power secrets were common knowledge. They won the enduros and motocrosses so they were what the sporting dirt or dual-purpose rider wanted.

Harley joined in, with a series of two-stroke singles Aermacchi built for the US market. The first adult version was the TX-125 in 1973. The engine was obviously descended from the older single but the TX had a full cradle frame, five speeds and oil injection (no more messy mixing of oil and gas).

Cycle World testers rode one and found it rode hard and shifted hard; they said the factory had a fix for the latter.

Road Rider's example hit 70, cruised at 55 and gave 55 mpg and 400 mpqt. of oil. (Shades of the early big twins.) There were some quirks, like the balky shift and not being able to check the battery when it was in the bike, but mostly the TX-125 had a full-sized chassis with a small engine, so it had to weigh 225 lb. and wasn't very fast.

No surprise, the 1974 model year brought the SX-175 along with the SX-125. (I don't know why the letter change.) One year after that came the SX-250; same theme, larger engine. Their gearboxes were faulty early in the model run and were replaced. If any escaped, they've surely broken by now, so the problem has been solved one way or another.

Cycle World weighed the SX-250 at 268 lb. and got 0-60 in 9.3 sec. and a quarter mile elapsed time of 16.89 sec. The 250 wasn't slow, nor especially fast, and the magazine said it made a good road bike but was outdated in the dirt.

In 1975 and 1976 the two-strokes came with choices of engine size and trim (SX for dual purpose, SS for street only). The ads said they were styled to resemble the Sport-

Year and model	1975 SX-250
Engine	two-stroke single
Bore and stroke	2.83x2.34 in.
Displacement	15 cu. in.
BHP	n/a
Gearbox	4 speeds
Shift	left foot
Wheelbase	54 in.
Wheels	21F/18R
Suspension	telescopic forks, swing-arm rear
Weight	268.5 lb., tank half full
Seat height	32.5 in.
MPG	n/a
Top speed	75 mph (est.)

The SX-250 was built in Italy and designed to counter Yamaha's DT-1, the street/trail two-stroke single that created a new market, in the US and abroad. The SX and TX Aermacchi Harleys had strong engines and competitive suspensions for their time, but they have since been surpassed. And as the only Harleys ever built to follow someone else's lead, they don't have much appeal as collector machines. Harley-Davidson photo.

ster and Super Glide and maybe they were, sort of.

Harley ads in 1977 hinted at what was to come: Buy an SS/SX125/175/250 and we'll throw in a portable radio, or a discounted camping trailer or a $100 rebate. When you're trying to sell what people don't want, you throw in something else. Evidently the program cleaned out the warehouses. The SX-250 was in the 1978 catalog, and this ended Harley's lightweight program.

What to look for

Once more, don't. The TX, SX and SS were okay, in their day, but now they aren't even average buys.

This isn't because of the machines themselves. Rather, there was a boom in trail bikes during the late sixties and early seventies, then the boom faded. Hundreds of thousands of such bikes were sold, then parked. For five hundred down to two hundred bucks you can get your choice of Harley, Honda, Kawasaki, Hodaka or Suzuki. You can ride the thing until it collapses, then buy another for less than you'd spend to repair the first one. A fine hobby, a lousy investment and, frankly, the Harleys are harder to find and more hassle to keep running until they expire.

Epilogue

So, what happened? If Harley-Davidson saw the future and was ready for it, why didn't the lightweight program work?

My explanation is snobbery, from all sides. People who wanted small motorcycles didn't want Harleys, were reluctant or even afraid to go inside a Harley store. People who rode Harleys didn't want small bikes. And the dealers didn't want low-margin machines, nor did they or their service departments understand the bikes or the people who bought them.

But you can't claim Harley-Davidson didn't try.

Chapter 6

Competition

★★★★★	KR, KRTT 1952-68
★★★★	KRM, KHR 1953-68
★★★	XLR 1957-69
★★★	? Iron XR-750 1969-71
★★	CRTT, CR, CRS 1961-67
★★★	Racing Aermacchis
★★★	RR-250 1971-77
★★	MX-250 1977-78
★★★★★	XR-750 1972-92

Real racing engines, a wise man once wrote, are engines next to which, when they're running, one is a little afraid to stand.

Harley-Davidson has built a lot of real racing engines. They had four-valve heads back in 1916, for instance, and won races around the world in the twenties and thirties. They were exotic and rare, and those that survive are treasured beyond price.

But just as interest in road motorcycles of the past has become a hobby for enthusiasts on a budget, so have racers of the more recent past sparked the formation of vintage racing clubs and the recognition of those clubs and classes by sanctioning bodies. Restoring old machines is fun and racing them gives us an excuse to do it.

My purpose here precludes discussion of the truly antique. I won't begin until the appearance of the KR racing Harley in 1952. But to appreciate that machine, we must look back to nearly twenty years before that.

The Depression put a damper on racing just as it did on everything else. Things got so tight there was only one factory, Harley-Davidson, with a racing department—and that was one man.

National championship racing had been open to pure racing machines, but one factory with one professional rider obviously wasn't going to be fair, nor would it draw crowds. So somebody came up with an Olympian ideal. The championship races would be contested on production bikes, modified versions of what was sold to the public. The factories wouldn't have an advantage and talent would tell.

Harley and Indian were both building 750 cc twins, and there were a handful of imports in the US, generally 500 cc singles. So these rules, defined in the American Motorcycle Association (AMA) regulations as Class C, set limits of 750 cc side valve, 500 cc overhead valve. (For the record, Classes A and B were the former professional classes, for dirt track and speedway.)

The new class worked fairly well. Overhead valve engines had more potential for power than flatheads, so the extra displacement evened things out. More guys could go racing and talent could appear; in fact, private tuners got more power from the stock-based engines than the factories did.

The ideal slipped only a little, in that Harley and Indian did eventually come to offer race-ready versions of the road bikes, rather than require everybody to buy the bike and strip it. But the rules did require the racing versions to be built from production engines.

KR and KRTT, 1952-68

When Harley came out with the K model in 1952, it was accompanied by a racing version, the KR.

It wasn't exactly the same engine. Same bore and stroke, same cases and barrels on the outside. But where the road-going K had roller bearings and bushings, the KR had ball bearings. Less friction equals more power. It also had hot cams, big valves, a magneto and tuned exhaust. And some very clever men spent thirty years flowing and shaping the ports and valves and combustion chambers. At first the K had 30 bhp and the KR, 38 to 40; by the time the KR went out of production, the archaic side valve would produce 62 bhp.

While the K was modern and had suspension at both ends, the KR had a rigid rear. And no brakes, because in those days brakes weren't allowed in flat-track racing. It sounds dangerous but in fact it wasn't. You can't stop fast on dirt anyway and the riders controlled speed by pitching the machines sideways. Tracks then were smooth and covered with loose dirt (the cushion, in racing parlance), and the brakeless, rigid-rear KR was a superb racing machine.

Enter another ideal. The national championship became a series of races, of different types. There were miles, half miles and short tracks (generally quarter miles), all flat ovals. There were road races, on pavement, and TT steeplechases, with jumps and with turns in both directions, but on dirt. (TT is short for Tourist Trophy, although how jumping and sliding in both directions in the dirt equates to tourism has been lost in time.)

A KR in its element: brakeless, sideways and wide open. Rider here is Bart Markel, AMA Grand National champion in 1962, 1965 and 1966. Harley-Davidson/Jerry Hatfield photo.

The racing KR was basically a stripped and souped version of the street Model K. Forks were the same, for instance, but the brake was taken off, while the engines looked alike on the outside but were very different inside. The dirt-only KR had a rigid rear wheel, held by a subframe that bolted to the main frame behind the seat and aft of the gearbox. The pad on the rear fender was there so the rider could shift his or her weight to the back for extra traction. Harley-Davidson photo.

Road racers, circa 1963. On the left is a KRTT, on the right, a CRTT. Both were adapted from road machines. KRTT rear suspension was shocks and swing arm bolted to the back of an old-style frame, with seat attached on top. CR had clip-on handlebars, road frame, massive four-shoe front brake. *Cycle World* photo.

Suspension was needed for TT and road racing. The regular KR used a smaller version of the K frame, but with a subframe making the rear frame junction, the rear axle and the swing arm a solid triangle. For TT and road courses there was a KR with shocks and drum brakes, known as the KRTT. There were conversion kits, KR to KRTT and back, as well as a road racing kit with fairing and big tank. There were big brakes and small brakes. The ideal here was that the national champion would be a rider who'd proved his skills on dirt and pavement, in sliding sideways and flying through the air, and he could do it on one motorcycle, by changing the rig between races.

Not a bad set up, and one in which the KR and KRTT did well. Tuners got more power every year. Even when Harley brought out the XL in place of the KH, the rules remained the same and the KR engine stayed in production.

The English got faster, and more powerful in AMA councils. The dirt tracks got rougher and rear suspension and brakes became the norm, culminating (for KR purposes) in a new KR frame in 1967. It was designed for rear suspension, and had a steering head closer to the ground, leading to the nickname Lowboy. This frame was all steel, with the top tubes extended to above the rear axle and triangulated with tubes from the swing arm pivot.

The Harley engine wasn't the best engine in racing at the time. The Harleys won the races and championships because the brand attracted some brilliant tuners, men who hadn't read the books and thus didn't know they couldn't get as much power from the outmoded design as they got. It was an odd situation but it made for good, close racing, which is what the sport is supposed to be about.

For instance, the best tuner was Tom Sifton, whose motors were so fast the factory couldn't match them, nor could it wheedle his secrets from him. Somebody told Sifton his bikes only won because the Harleys were bigger, so he built a BSA 500 and beat the other BSAs, and the factory Harleys.

I digress. In 1968 the English got the upper hand and the AMA changed the rules —okay, modernized them—into Class C meaning a 750 cc limit, no valve configuration mentioned. And the production ideal had evolved into the factory being required

KR barrel, slightly the worse for wear. Shape of relief, leading the incoming and outgoing charge from valves next to bore, was critical.

Even in road racing trim (big tank, fairing and Sportster brakes), the KRTT's ancestry is obvious. The sprung seat and pad (for when the rider crouched on the tank down the straights) are pure dirt track. Harley-Davidson photo.

to make two hundred examples of the model and offering them for general sale.

Harley-Davidson wasn't quite ready. It made an interim model, the first (iron) XR-750 for 1970, and began on the second (alloy) XR-750. In the 1969 Daytona 200, first match of the dumb old flathead versus equally big ohv English twins, the KRTT was home first, a winner to the end.

What to look for

Simply finding a KR or KRTT will be the first step. The people who built them estimate there were between 1,000 and 1,500 racing machines built between 1952 and 1968. But you hardly ever see them now.

This may be due to attrition. The flathead engine was stressed beyond normal limits and when it blew, which it did a lot, it blew in a big way. The engine was often destroyed, so the rolling chassis was pushed into a corner until somebody put a Sportster engine in it.

Further, a lot of the racers then really loved the sport and they've held on to the old machines and they aren't for sale; some of the true enthusiasts, Roger Reiman for example, still race their old flatheads. And for complicated legal reasons there can be several engines with the same number. Buying a certified winner of a race or a series can tax even the expert: Beginners, Beware.

Next, models. There were rigid KRs. There were early KRTTs with cast-iron frame junctions and rigid rear frame sections. And later, KRTTs with all-steel frames. There were road racers with fairings, first allowed in 1963, and later fairings as seen on the

The 1966 KRTT was an interim model, in that there was a streamlined seat and tank and a separate rear brake, on the old-style frame. When the magneto went to the generator's normal home, the old magneto drive was used for the tachometer drive. Harley-Davidson photo.

factory bikes in 1968 and 1969. There were big brakes and small brakes, and a handful of late KR engines had dual carbs.

Further, there's the problem of authenticity. K and KR engines look more alike than they are. Check the pad on the left half of the crankcase, between the cylinder bases. If it says plain K, not KR, it may have been built into a KR, but it was not originally a KR.

Year and model	1963 KR-TT (road racer)
Engine	side valve 45° V-twin
Bore and stroke	2.75x3.81 in.
Displacement	45 cu. in.
BHP	48 (claimed)
Gearbox	4 speeds
Shift	right foot
Wheelbase	56 in.
Wheels	19 in. (18 optional)
Suspension	telescopic forks, swing-arm rear
Weight	396 lb., tank half full
Seat height	30 in.
MPG	depended on gearing
Top speed	140 mph (geared for road racing)

Remember, this stuff has been mixed and matched for thirty years, and most of the clubs don't care too much. But it's best if the seller can prove he's got what he says he's got.

Parts. If the KR used a part that was also on the K or KH or XL or XLR or XR, no problem, it's out there. The rest are used. Again, it will take an expert eye. There's nothing that can't be found, duplicated or substituted. It will just take longer.

Rating: For experts only

When vintage racing began in the early 1980s, there was *a* vintage race during Cycle Week at Daytona Beach.

There's no such thing as a stock racing bike. This KRTT has the last of the engine mods, dual carbs, Ceriani forks and four-shoe drum front brake. The frame, though, especially around the steering head and the rear top tubes, doesn't look factory.

In 1992, there was a full day of vintage racing. Better than 400 entries, with more classes that there's space to list here.

This tremendous interest alone guarantees that every KR still in existence will be hunted down, dragged out of the back of the cellar or barn and restored.

That's not strong enough. There's already been one production run of replica KRTT, that is, road racing, frames since the boom began. There's a nice chap who'll make you any of the fairings or tanks the KRTTs ever wore. And because there were more engines than frames, within a short time span I bet there will be more old KRs than there were new ones.

For this reason alone, we'll rate the KR and KRTT at five stars.

Now comes the cautions. The best known examples, the KRTTs made by and raced by the factory team, are accounted for. They will command the highest price when you buy, and perhaps when you sell. But watch yourself. The car people have already demonstrated that somehow replicas of famous models come on the market, um, confused with the originals.

Further, these engines are witchcraft. Clearances and settings are critical. Put a wrench wrong and it's Blanggg! all over the track. Even done right, a KR engine has a working life measured in hours. Don't buy

This KRTT shows line of descent: Cases, engine mounts, primary cover are obviously related to the K and Sportster. That's the post-1967 Lowboy frame and single carb, but the fairing is an adaptation.

one and expect to ride it to work. If you want a hot flathead Harley, go for the KK or KHK instead.

KRM and KHR, 1953-68

While the national championship was based on the Class C formula, production-based, 750 cc limit, not all races were for that championship and not all racing bikes met those limits.

Back when there were 74 and 80 in. road bikes, there was an open class or an 80 in. class, generally for hillclimbs and TTs. And in the west there were the desert races.

So, when the K became the KH, Harley offered clubman racers, the KHR and KHRTT. All the other specifications apply here (rigid rear frame section, brakes or no brakes, ball bearing mains), except that the KHR had the different flywheels, taller barrels and longer stroke of the KH.

Perhaps because the major magazines were in the west and tended to pay more attention to the desert races, where the Triumphs and BSAs did well, Harley announced a mix of K and KR in 1953.

It was called the KRM. It was a scrambler, with no lights but with a skid plate to protect the engine. It had the tuned, KK engine. According to *Cycle* magazine the KRM weighed 50 lb. more than the English

The old master. This is Roger Reiman on his factory team KRTT with full fairing, streamlined seat, disc rear and four-shoe front brakes. Reiman is an Illinois Harley dealer. Before that he won the Daytona 200 in 1964 and 1965 and was national champ in 1964.

competition, and the Harley factory failed to persuade the desert stars to ride one.

All the above warnings apply here, and so does the four-star rating, I guess, because if you found one it would be rare indeed and there's usually value in that.

Good luck.

XLR, 1957-69

When the XL Sportster replaced the KH, the KHR was replaced by a monster known as the XLR. As the letters hint, this was a racing version of the Sportster engine, just as the KR was to the K.

The XLR had the XL's bore and stroke of 3.05x3.812 in., the same 883 cc/54 cu. in. displacement and the same basic cases, barrels and heads. Inside, though, were ball bearings and special valvetrain. A vertical magneto replaced the generator, and the heads had bigger valves and ports. Technically the XLR is also the XLRTT because it was built mostly for TT racing and had rear suspension.

The XLR is reported to have produced 82 bhp. Joe Leonard and his XLR held the Ascot TT record for years. One example appeared in European road races and did well. I call it a monster because that's a lot of power for those early frames.

What to look for

Dick O'Brien, who ran Harley's racing department from 1957 until 1983 and who should know about this, says more than 500 XLRs were built.

What he doesn't know is where they all are now. I've seen a handful of genuine, certified examples. I've seen decals gathering dust on parts counters and I know guys who have spare parts. I can even recall one XLR offered for sale during the past five years.

Finding an XLR won't be easy. If you think you have one, check the cases. They should be stamped XLR. Insist on looking inside, to be sure the main bearings are ball bearings, and that the crankpin is larger than the XL crankpin. Don't be put off by the kick

KRM was supposed to be a desert racer. In effect it was the KR engine, with all speed equipment, in a stripped K frame. It had brakes and suspension but no lights or mufflers. The KRM was seldom seen in 1954, less so now. Harley-Davidson photo.

Harley doesn't like sudden changes. The XLR had different cases from the KR but the primary cover, magneto and mag drive, oil tank and a host of minor bits were the same, and could interchange. Harley-Davidson photo.

HARLEY
DAVIDSON

lever; both XLR and KHR had kick start. An XL engine in an XLR or KR frame would be fun, it's just that you don't want to pay factory prices for a homemade machine.

Some of the parts are surprisingly available. The crankpin uses the same rollers and cages as the later XR750, for instance, and clutch plates, primary drive and gasket are just like on the early XL.

Rating: Three stars

Here's a case of the mousetrap being better than the mice deserve. An XLR doesn't fit vintage racing rules. Nobody will recognize it as a show example. And you'd be better off on the road with a stripped-down early XLCH.

An XLR would be rewarding to locate and restore only for the inner-directed collector. Nobody else will have ever heard of the bike, much less appreciate it.

Iron XR-750, 1969-71

Don't let me get the bit in my teeth, okay? I own one of these and have acquired a few thousand more facts about it than you need to know.

When the AMA changed the national championship rules in late 1968, allowing 750s of all types to compete against each other, Harley-Davidson needed time to build a truly competitive engine.

So it made do, by de-stroking the XLR engine. The first XR-750 had the 3.00 in. bore of the XL883 and XLR, but the stroke was 3.219 in., instead of 3.812, to meet the 750 cc limit. The XR used the same basic flywheels as the XLR but with the giant crankpin closer to the center, so close that the nuts for the

The XLRTT was a full-race version of the Sportster 883 engine, sold with brakes and suspension but without lights or street equipment. It was used mostly for nonchampionship events. Several hundred were made, a few stock examples may still exist. Harley-Davidson photo.

mainshafts interfered with the crankpin. The problem was solved (almost) by pressing the shafts into the wheels, rather than bolting them in. (I say "almost" because the shafts came loose. The factory welded later flywheels, then installed a nut on the other side, then finally forged one-piece flywheels. Wish I could find a set, but I promised not to bore you with my troubles.)

Connecting rods were shared with the XLR, barrels were cut-down XL examples and the pistons in the first engines began their lives intended for use in the Offenhauser 1500 cc midget engine. Of course there were hot cams and a magneto mounted where the XL had a generator. Suspension was universal by 1969 so the XR was also an XRTT; it had the 1967 frame with full suspension, Girling shocks in back, Ceriani forks in front. The baseline model came minus brakes but they could be ordered for TT, as could a big tank and full fairing for road racing. Claimed dry weight in mile trim, with 2.25 gal. tank, was 320 lb. Mine, with triple disc brakes as per TT, generator, tiny mufflers and full tank, weighs 365 lb.

The iron XR-750 wasn't a success. It was slower than the English bikes, never mind getting its fiberglass blown off at Daytona in 1970 by the Honda four. The XR was at first slower than the KR, and when the XR made power it also made stupendous quantities of heat. Gene Romero (Triumph) won the AMA title in 1970 and Dick Mann (BSA) won it in 1971. The alloy engine of 1972 didn't come any too soon.

What to look for

The rules required at least two hundred examples to be made and counted. This was done. What Harley didn't do was sell that many. The bike didn't win, so privateers didn't buy and even the team guys relied on the old KR. The leftovers were scrapped for tax write-offs.

Directly or indirectly I've knowledge of somewhere between twelve and twenty of the engines still in existence. Doubtless there are more, but there can't be many.

The average fan can't spot the difference between an early XR and a Sportster, but it's easy: The XR cases are stamped 1C, followed

Original XR-750 had iron barrels, heads and de-stroked XLR engine and used the Lowboy-style KRTT frame. It was introduced in 1970 and was raced by the factory team during that year and in 1971. It wasn't a success. Harley-Davidson photo.

by the actual serial number, followed by H0. The 1C surely must represent the first competition series, and H0 is tenth year, seventh decade.

Don't worry if the barrels have XL numbers. The XR used XL barrels with 0.30 in. whacked off the top. Count the fins; the XR has eleven, the XL has twelve.

For the other worries, refer to the KR and XLR. I have stuff on my bike that isn't XR and I don't care because it works. And if you tackle this or any other racing bike, be sure you have at least two of the following three: patience, skill as a machinist, piles of money.

Rating: Three (?) stars

Skepticism is warranted here because the iron XR wasn't great in its day, and the vintage rules don't like it now. You run Formula 750 class, against those Triumph triples and Honda fours that whipped the XR when new. They still will.

But that hasn't stopped the bidding. The first XR I saw for sale had an asking price of $2,000. Next one was $4,500, and early in 1985 there was an ad for a street-legal XR for $7,500, which is much too much.

A team XR-750 in full road race trim, maybe. But these were the dirt version. All the XRs have been discovered, or at least they're beginning to be known, and speculation is already under way, which makes them less sensible as an investment. I wouldn't sell mine, not for $7,000, not for $17,000. But mine was a labor of love, not an investment.

CRTT, CR and CRS, 1961-67

Bless the rule makers. About the time small but real motorcycles appeared in the US, racing classes were designed for them

By 1970 the Aermacchi single had evolved into a real racer, as in full fairing, streamlined seat and tank. This is the 350 sold to privateers in Europe. *Cycle World* photo.

and the rules, like those for the big bikes, required production-based components.

So with the Sprint and Sprint H and C, there came the CR, CRTT and CRS, racing versions of the Italian-made 250 cc single.

I suspect no two were alike. They divided first into two versions, one for short track and novice racing, the other for road racing in what was then the lightweight class. There were the early versions, with the long-stroke engine, wet clutch and mostly the production parts lightened and modified, but when the short-stroke 250 came out, the R in that version had a dry clutch and extensive reworking of the engine's internals. The CR and CRS were the dirt versions, and had less exotic parts than the CRTT road racers with their five-speed gearboxes and outside flywheels. Before 1966 the frames were steel, but after that they were steel and aluminum.

What to look for

This isn't a job for the layman. There were about seven hundred CRs made in various forms, but I don't know how many were customer model dirt racers and how many were factory-backed road racers. Nor can you or I just look at the combinations created over the years and know what came from what, not until we've studied the machines.

Parts are tough. The Harley-Aermacchis were built in Europe as road racers and are

Later Aermacchi Sprint-based CRTT bore little resemblance to the street scramblers, what with the new tank and seat, the alloy plates for engine mounts and the reworked head with vertical intake port. That's the short-stroke engine.

Year and model	1963 CR-TT (road racer)
Engine	ohv single
Bore and stroke	2.59x2.83 in.
Displacement	15 cu. in.
BHP	28 (claimed)
Gearbox	4 speeds
Shift	right foot
Wheelbase	52 in.
Wheels	18 in.
Suspension	telescopic forks, swing-arm rear
Weight	245 lb., tank full
Seat height	28 in.
MPG	depended on gearing
Top speed	116 mph (observed)

still raced in Formula classes in England and Europe, which is where the best of the most rare parts are—some new, some replica. A guy who's just restored a CRTT says he worked so long and hard that he may not race the bike because he can't stand the thought of finding another missing or broken piece.

Rating: For you, two

Or me. Vintage racing is what these machines are good for and that limits what the enthusiast can do with one. Moreso, the dirt track vintage clubs sometimes require the rider to have demonstrated some ability, or raced before. Short track is tough to learn when you're old enough to shave.

Road racing, as in the CRTT, is less demanding. What this comes to here is, you'll pay close to five figures for a really competitive CRTT in class-winning form, at least a grand for a tired and tacky short tracker.

Add it all up and unless you're really keen on vintage road racing and have spare time and are willing to comb through the old books and badger the guys who built and raced the CRs, they're of less than average value when it comes to investing.

Racing Aermacchis

While serving as Harley's junior varsity in the United States, Aermacchi had its own successful racing effort in Europe.

Its first production racer was a version of the road-going 250, with tuned engine, racing tires and rear-set seat and pegs. In keeping with Aermacchi's system of the time it was called the Ala d'Oro, or Gold Wing. (Honda paid to use the name on its later touring machine.)

The Ala d'Oro was the European equivalent of the CRTT. When the engine got a bigger bore and shorter stroke (still 250 cc), an outside flywheel and five speeds, it became the DS. The third version was DS-S and finally, in 1968, it was called DS-S2.

The road engine grew to 350 cc in the United States and Europe. There was no American class for the 350 then, but there was interest overseas so Aermacchi offered a customer racer, the DS-S350.

What to look for

Each version of the Aermacchi production racer was quicker and faster and better than the one before. And all the models meet vintage or formula racing rules in Europe and the United Kingdom.

So first, haunt the paddock at vintage races, taking notes and pictures until you can spot the real versus replica and new versus old. Then hunt for the most authentic and the newest.

Rating: Three stars

The racing Aermacchis were, and still are, winners. This also means they're known values; the very best ones, the former team 350s with shorter-than-stock stroke and bigger bore and more power, now sell for collector prices, which brings the prices of the lesser models up as well. So they're a safe investment albeit there's scant hope of turning a quick or impressive profit.

RR-250, 1971-77

Road racing went through major changes in the late sixties and early seventies, just as dirt track did. In Europe the Japanese arrived, conquered, backed off and came back again, while four-strokes were replaced by two-strokes.

Aermacchi was active in racing there and then, first with air-cooled two-stroke twins and later with water-cooled versions of the same engine. These were good bikes. Walter Villa won the world 250 title in 1974, 1975 and 1976, and the 350 title in 1976. Harley offered customer versions of this machine, homologated in the United States as the RR250/350.

RR-250 was a pure road racing motorcycle, powered by a 250 cc two-stroke twin that had no relationship to any other engine made by Harley or Aermacchi. It was built to compete in world and US races and it did well. They're rare now and while you can get the parts, they can't be used for anything except racing and current rules make them too slow for real races, too new for vintage classes. Only experts need apply, in other words. Harley-Davidson photo.

But by the time the American models arrived, they were outclassed by the Yamaha 350s and the classes had changed. Gary Scott and Jay Springsteen rode RR-250s. But they didn't win titles with them.

Year and model	1976 RR-250
Engine	two-stroke twin
Bore and stroke	56x50 mm
Displacement	15 cu. in.
BHP	53 (claimed)
Gearbox	5 speeds
Shift	right foot
Wheelbase	55 in.
Wheels	18 in.
Suspension	telescopic forks, swing-arm rear
Weight	259 lb., tank half full
Seat height	n/a
MPG	13 to 15
Top speed	125 mph (observed)

What to look for

Exactly how many RR-250s are around, nobody knows. I have seen a few for sale, usually with spare parts and for a reasonable price, a few grand. As for authenticity there shouldn't be any problem because an RR-250 can't be anything else. Nothing else fits, unlike the KR or XR.

Rating: Three shakey stars

Discouragement is encouraged. An RR-250 will be even more tricky than a KR.

The MX-250 was competitive when new but the more expensive and advanced motocrossers from Japan drove it off the track and off the market. Harley-Davidson photo.

Nor can an RR-250 be converted for the road or ridden as anything except a racing machine. And I doubt there were more than the required twenty-five made, never mind actually sold.

On the other hand, as they get older, the RR-250s are becoming eligible for vintage road racing and they will probably be capable of wins in the right hands.

More important for our short-term outlook, an example went for big bucks at the auction in Daytona Beach in 1992. Next I knew there were calls from owners and potential owners looking for ways to authenticate their machines because they were suddenly worth big bucks.

For the ordinary fan looking for a motorcycle to play with, uh-uh. But if you stumble across an RR-250 and can scoop it up, it will almost surely be worth your effort.

MX-250, 1977-78

Aermacchi's experience with two-strokes stood the company in good stead for road machines, trail bikes and motocross in the seventies. Harley was able to import 250 cc motocross racers for its own team and for private sale.

But that was then. Since then, Harley has stopped importing the Italian bikes, has in fact sold Aermacchi back to Italian investors, who in turn have made the new firm, named Cagiva, the largest in Europe. Cagiva now makes excellent motocross and enduro bikes, which bear no relationship at all to the old MX-250s.

What to look for

Another negative. The MX-250 is completely outdated and outclassed. All you'll find is a tired old dirt bike, no longer raced because it can't win.

Rating: Two firm stars

Motocross is for youth, machines as well as people. Dirt bikes get old fast. There are

The alloy XR-750 had new heads and cylinders, dual carbs, less weight and more power. The configuration of the engine was the same as the iron XR, XL, K and so on. This is a 1972 model, brakeless and thus set up for the mile or half mile. Harley-Davidson photo.

some old Harley MX-250s around. There are more outmoded Honda, Yamaha, Suzuki and Kawasaki motocrossers around, all for a few hundred bucks—and good luck when you get them home.

Motocross bikes make terrible play-bikes. If you want something to bang around in the woods or the dirt, fine. Get an older enduro model from the big four. Ride it, break it and buy another. But don't try it on an old Harley two-stroke. Like the tiddlers before them, the MX-250s should be allowed to wear out and return to mother earth.

XR-750, 1972-92

Back to optimism. Harley-Davidson took some lumps in 1970-71 but in 1972 produced the alloy XR-750, one of the most successful racers of all time.

The Olympian ideal, meanwhile, had suffered some erosion. A factory wishing to contest for the national championship was now required only to make 200 engines available to the general public, rather than 200 complete machines.

So the new XR needn't have looked anything like the XL engine. But it did. The cases looked alike, the engine mounts were the same and some parts, for example the clutch sprocket and primary chain and primary cover gasket, will interchange with the early Sportster.

But there the similarities end. The new XR has alloy heads with improved combustion chambers and dual carbs. The alloy barrels were massively finned. The engine set a record; the 3.125 in. bore was larger than the 2.983 in. stroke—the first oversquare Harley ever and the third set of dimensions for the factory's fourth 750 cc racing V-twin. Primary drive, timing case and gearbox were

Most XRs were sold ready for dirt track. The heritage of that first K can still be seen—in the primary cover and engine mounts, for example. The exhaust ports were both at the front, for better cooling. Harley-Davidson photo.

pretty much the same, while the flywheels, connecting rods, crankpin, pistons, valves and rocker boxes were all different. Nor would they interchange.

This engine went into the old frame, just as Harley did with road machines, and the complete bikes were sold minus brakes but naturally with suspension. And you could get the brakes, heaps of different gears, even road racing tank, fairing, clip-on bars, the works.

The new XR drove first the Triumph, BSA and Norton teams out of American dirt track. Then it whipped the Yamaha vertical twins. When Yamaha came back with a V-twin, the Harley whomped it some more. It drubbed Honda's adapted 750, the cross-mount CX500 turned in the frame.

But, as Custer's welcoming committee used to say, only earth and sky are forever. Honda doesn't like to lose. It bought an XR, shipped it home and returned with its own V-twin, fore and aft, same bore and stroke but with four valves per cylinder, overhead cams and, well, just about every improvement you could make to an eleven-year-old engine if you had the money. Honda won the title, as the company heads had vowed to do.

But there was some politicking, rule changes involving weight and carb sizes and

Year and model	1978 XR-750 (dirt tracker)
Engine	ohv 45° V-twin
Bore and stroke	3.125x2.98 in.
Displacement	45 cu. in.
BHP	90 (est.)
Gearbox	4 speeds
Shift	right foot
Wheelbase	57 in.
Wheels	19 in. (18 optional)
Suspension	telescopic forks, swing-arm rear
Weight	320 lb., tank full
Seat height	31 in.
MPG	n/a
Top speed	130 mph (geared for mile oval)

Road racing XRs had seat, tank and brakes almost identical to the late KRTTs, but of course with the alloy ohv engine. Yamaha brought out the TZ700, the AMA changed the rules to make 25 engines a production run and the Harley twins (along with all the other four-stroke twins) disappeared from road racing. An XR like this is rare and expensive. Harley-Davidson photo.

such. Honda lost interest and Harley-Davidson kept on working. The result was a revised engine, with new and improved ports and valve signalled by a D-shaped intake port and the Harley team took back the lead. At this writing, 1992, there's no rival in sight.

What to look for

Finding an XR-750 is as easy as picking up a copy of *Cycle News*. About six hundred of them have been made. There are several hundred licensed AMA experts and as many AMA juniors. They all need a Harley 750 for the miles and half miles. So people are always selling, buying, trading and retiring them. There's always an XR for sale near you.

Guys like former racer and national champion Mert Lawwill, former factory wrench Steve Storz and flamboyant privateer tuner Tex Peel build bikes faster than the factory's. They design and sell parts and there are more frames, cams, heads, ignitions, pipes, suspensions and brakes than can be described here.

You won't find a stock machine. Not ever. Nor will you not know an XR when you see one, because there's nothing like it. All the parts are available, in theory, from your local H-D store. But if the parts man won't help, a racer-oriented shop can.

Professional racing is one, big, friendly but competitive family. You won't be looking for this or that part. Instead, you'll find ads for national runners—which means a good rider can make the main event—down to "junior" bikes, which have restricted carbs and generally not the latest speed goodies. You can tell which is which because of the

In its element, the alloy XR-750, ridden here by three-time national champion Jay Springsteen, in the 1979 TT National in Houston's Astrodome. Harley-Davidson photo.

price, higher for the faster bikes. Buyers and sellers generally know each other so it's hard for the price to be out of line.

Age doesn't matter. My frame was made in 1972, revised in 1975. One just like it, made and revised at the same time, won national races in 1982. Condition—how many hours on the engine—is more important.

Rating: Five bright stars

This begins our silver lining. An alloy XR-750 is a contemporary racing machine. In the right hands it can earn somebody a living. So we aren't looking at recognizing worth the rest of the world doesn't appreciate.

But business works in racing the way it works in business. The constant improvement of the basic package, especially the major rework for the D-port heads and new material used in the 1990 cases, means the pros have to buy new parts and upgrade, which costs them.

For the racer this means extra expense, having to buy new engines and learn how to make them work.

For the collector, this means the current engines will begin to depreciate, if they haven't already. The past is prologue, as somebody wrote. Racing machines are always expensive when new, then they're outmoded and cheap, then they're rare and gain value again. Check the prices on old Ferraris or board-track Indians or Manx Nortons.

Right, you may be thinking, but what do I do with this racer while I wait for the return on my investment?

Ride it.

If you have some common sense, extra time, patience and the willingness to learn.

You can't race it, not in real races, because you haven't got a license and you aren't a good enough rider, no offense.

But the XR has a hidden asset. Where the KR and the first XR had ball bearings, the current XR has Superblend bearings, odd things shaped like little beer kegs. They last longer. The experts tell me a carefully built, ridden and maintained XR should have an engine life of 20,000 to 30,000 miles. This means you can go places on it and ride it for a few years between rebuilds.

Next, the heritage. Because the cases are based on the XL engine, you can put a generator where the XR magneto used to be, and add the kick start from an XLR, lights from a Sportster and so on. It ain't easy. I got my major parts late in 1980, figured to run the vintage class at Daytona (mine's iron, don't forget, old enough for the class) in 1981. I got there in 1985.

Right. There's no place for luggage, no room for a passenger. You'll have to stop for gas every 100 miles but that won't matter because your kidneys will be pounded and your teeth loosened by then anyway. Firm is how an XR rides, and it needs a firm hand on the reins because it's supposed to turn.

While you're waiting to make money, you'll have the best motorcycle Harley-Davidson never sold.

Chapter 7

People and Places

Now that we've charted all the territory, so to speak, it's time to see how we actually go about finding all the winners previously described, and to look at what to do when we've found them.

The used bike market

Where you look naturally depends on what you're after. The easiest way to find a late-model road machine is to check your local newspaper. Every one worthy of the name has classified ads, sometimes even with the makes in alphabetical order. When you get that far, as in seeing an ad for "1977 FLH, Fully Dressed, Lo Mi Nu Trs, $4,500 obo," all you need to do is call the owner and check out the bike. Of course, you already have your license, so you can ride the machine before you buy, and if you aren't a technician you'll take along a friend who is.

The next best hunting ground is the Harley-Davidson store. Like any new-vehicle dealer, Harley takes in trades and the good ones generally are on display. You might even luck into an unsold model from the previous year, on which the dealer may be willing to negotiate. While you're there, visit the parts department and look for a bulletin board. Most dealerships let their customers tack up ads for older bikes and/or parts. The bulletin board is also a good place to learn about swap meets, races, road runs, field meets and other events.

Independent repair shops do the same thing. My neighborhood shop (which deals in Harleys and dirt bikes because the owner is a retired racer who's building up a Panhead) currently has two Sportsters on consignment and there's an ad for another on the board. Further, if you're in the market for an early Electra Glide or a Sprint or whatever, tell the man behind the counter. He may know somebody who wants to sell but hasn't bothered to advertise, or where an old one is parked.

Really old or competition bikes are harder to find. The best general source is *Cycle News*, the weekly racing paper. Check the rack at the dealership or parts store or write one of its offices. A subscription currently goes for $50 a year, fifty issues.

Cycle News
PO Box 498
Long Beach, CA 90801-0498

The vintage, collection and nostalgia boom have done wonders for the specialist press. One of the originals is:

Old Time Cycles
8280 Janes Avenue
Woodridge, IL 60517

They have lots of ads, Harleys and Indians and the others, plus reprints of tests and if you subscribe you get a free ad.

Brand new—the premier issue appeared in March, 1992—is:

Motorcycle Collector
30011 Ivy Glenn Drive, Ste. 114
Laguna Niguel, CA 92677

Editor and publisher is Don Emde, winner of the Daytona 200 but he won't tell you unless you ask. Knows his stuff, though, and the magazine will have ads and tech tips and parts leads and so forth.

If you can ignore an old rivalry, you might enjoy:
Iron Trader News
P.O. Box 8679
Pittsburgh, PA 15221

They specialize in American V-twins, which means Harley-Davidson and of course Indian—by now it's safe to like both, by the way. And the magazine, which comes out six times a year for $16, also gets you a free ad, covers dirt track racing current and vintage and has tech tips and sources for parts.

Racing fans will need the *Harley Competition Network*. This was begun by a man who owns an XR-750 and wanted to share info and parts. He began a register and it grew into a pocket-sized newsletter. Good place to pick up data, not to mention a KR or an XLCR or a rolling chassis with either stock or Lawwill frames. It's $12 for six issues or $15 for six issues with free ads.
Competition Harley Network
1355 Kingsdale
Hoffman Estates, IL 60194
The subscription also entitles you to run an ad, up to 100 words, for no extra charge.
Old Time Cycles
8280 Janes Ave.
Woodridge, IL 60517

New Englanders can find rare motorcycles in *Motorcyclist's Post*. This unusual news-

Waiting to hurry up, this aggregate of dressers and Sportys will in a few minutes form the annual motorcycle parade at Daytona Beach.

paper is a mix of local race results, club meets and old-time stuff, sort of an inner circle and not terribly exciting unless you're inside the circle. But it does list bikes and parts for old Harleys (and Indians, fair is fair) and upcoming events.

Motorcyclist's Post
PO Box 154
Rochdale, MA 01542

Sources for parts

Harley-Davidson has been good about keeping parts in supply over the years, so your dealership is the place to begin. A concern here may be that the nearest agency isn't the closest source. The dealership nearest me is friendly but it doesn't have as many parts as does the shop that's fifty miles in the other direction; consequently I trade with the independent shop a mile down the street. All one can say here is, it depends.

Because Harleys stay on the road forever, and because the policy of gradual change has made it economic for outsiders to supply parts, there are excellent sources outside the dealer network.

Really older machines need special attention, in the form of mail order. Mostly these are companies that have bought out dealerships and stockpiled obsolete parts in the hope that people like us would come looking, which we are beginning to do.

Antique Cycle Supply is one of the big ones. It catalogs parts for Harley twins from 1915 through 1985, with emphasis on the E and F models. Some of the stock is from former dealerships, some is reproduced and some comes from government surplus. It also has shop tools and literature, helpful for the restorer. A catalog costs $5.

You can get anything you want, but you'll have to search for it. This is the used parts wall at Insane Wayne's 45 Harley Shop. Those are primary, timing case and sprocket covers.

Antique Cycle Supply, Inc.
Cedar Springs, MI 49319
(616) 636-8200

Sometimes the dealer is slow. In those cases, I've had good luck with
Lake Shore Harley-Davidson
1424 Belvedere Rd.
Waukegan, IL 60085

They have a toll-free 'phone line (800) 322-5272 and they ship every day and they have most modern parts, or at least so it's proven when I've called them.

For the *really tough* parts hunts, the place is
Finders Service
454-458 West Lincoln Highway
Chicago Heights, IL 60411

During their forty years, they say, they've found ninety-eight percent of the parts they've been asked to find. Their procedure can be a bother, as they require details and the parts numbers used by the factory and sometimes a deposit or earnest money so nobody's time is wasted. When you need to get the part, it's worth it.

A sort of side note here is that the rear engine mount for iron XLs and XRs or all type was weak when it appeared in 1957 and didn't get any better. Besides, it's nearly impossible to replace when it breaks, which it may well do. The cure is an infinitely better mount, from
Pringle Enterprises
Rte. 1, Box 423C
Adams, WI 53910

Vintage and perhaps even contemporary racers need to know about
Schafer Fiberglass Racing Products
P.O. Box 388
Troutman, NC 28166

On display, row after row of restored or preserved motorcycles. This is from the Visalia meet, one of the West Coast's biggest. David Gooley photo.

They make fiberglass fuel tanks, seats, fairings and tail sections for early and late KR and XR road racers and flat track machines.

There are specialists. My favorite is the 45 Harley Shop, run by a chap who calls himself Insane Wayne. He deals in K, KH and KR parts, mostly used, with a sideline in whatever other Harley components turn up. And he always seems to know where you can find what he doesn't have.
45 Harley Shop
10020 Prospect Ave., Suite A-12
Santee, CA 92071
(619) 448-7139

This list is far from complete. I could make it more complete by whipping through a copy of *Old Time Cycles* and culling the ads but I don't know most of the people involved and thus hesitate to recommend them. The burden is on you, but the parts are there if you look.

The best source of parts and information for the Aermacchi-built road racing machines is racer/enthusiast Dick Linton at FLC Imports in the UK.
FLC Imports
Telford House
Little Mead
Cranleigh, Surrey UK
04866 5868

Cagiva Motor SpA is a good source of major technical parts for the later two-strokes.
Cagiva Motor SpA
via G Macchi
144 Schiranna
21100 Varese, Italy

Swap meets have things you may need, or may not be able to identify. In the foreground is the skeleton of an Indian Chief, late model because it's got plunger hubs and springer forks. What the other flywheels, barrels and fenders belong to, only a collector could tell. David Gooley photo.

Another good source is the counter of your neighborhood parts store. Many companies make Harley parts. Most of them aren't mail order. Instead, the parts stores and repair shops have the catalog. You look up what you want, then the store orders it for you. Gary Bang is probably the best for reproduction parts for older twins; Jammer, Drag Specialties and S&S concern themselves with custom, as in chopper, gear. But as restoration becomes more popular and the Japanese customs infringe on the outlaw look, the chopper suppliers are more willing to provide replacement girder forks, frames and such.

I should include here the straight equipment people, Barnett, Sifton et al, who specialize in gears or clutches or cables. If the man behind the counter deserves to be there, he'll know which catalog to thumb through. (Personally, I have little experience with the names listed above. I can vouch for Arlen Ness, whose parts are of excellent quality, and for SuperTrapp exhaust systems, but in general I haven't bought enough from these catalogs to know who's good and who's not.)

Also a good hunting ground are the pages of magazines reporting on Harleys. *Hot Bike* is the most technically oriented and *Easy Rider* has the most pages, albeit most of their coverage is of the, um, human element. Sorry to sound like a prude, but some of the material in the chopper mags isn't suitable for children.

However, if you flip past the color sections—or enjoy them, what do I care?—there are lots of ads for cases, frames, front end parts, tanks and so on.

Swap meets are another world. Some are mostly commercial, with outmoded junk that didn't sell the first time around, and used parts to which the holder may have title.

The gimlet-eyed author in a slow race. This is where all the bikes start across a line and the last one to get to the finish line 100 feet away with feet still off the ground, wins. (I won this heat, and was second in the final. Better luck next time.) David Gooley photo.

Others are invaluable: Guys who saved what everybody else pitched out years ago show up with truckloads of tarnished and rusted pieces not even they can identify. If all you need to complete the restoration is the battery box for your EL or the backing plate for the front brake of your XLCH, this may be the only place you'll find it.

Finding the swap meet can be as difficult as finding the part. Some daily newspapers list meets, so do club bulletins, but most of the time you'll do best by keeping an eye on the dealer's bulletin board.

Philosophical note: It might be possible not only to assemble a complete old Harley from NOS (new-old-stock) parts, it might be possible to do it without using one component that came from the H-D factory.

This could be a problem. If you're assembling, restoring or maintaining a motorcycle just to ride or tinker with, you won't care. But if you'll be showing the bike or have an eye on its value, be informed here that the judges will mark against the machine if, say, it's a Knucklehead with Panhead barrels, or an early Shovelhead engine in a Panhead frame. They may be even tougher on a reproduction frame wearing made-outside-America fenders and tanks.

Now, I'm not saying don't do it. If using barrels from here on cases from there is the only way to have a running engine, why, do it! Just don't be surprised if it's held against you.

Reading material

As you have surely surmised, this book isn't complete; that is, it doesn't contain every fact known to Harley riders and builders. Not possible here.

The hoop toss. They drape bicycle tires over your shoulders, then you ride down a line and fling the tires over (more like at) the cones set on another line. It's no easier than it looks. David Gooley photo.

However, when it comes to your machine, you can't know too much. For late-model stockers, the Harley store will have a shop manual that should tell you everything you need to know. Failing that, Clymer and Haynes offer manuals, usually stocked at the parts counter.

Going older and deeper, the independent shops carry an excellent series of collected technical data. Called *Shop Dope*, it's books filled with all the factory bulletins issued over the years, from 1936 to the present. The volumes are by era rather than model. Thus they contain tips not of concern, for the flathead big twins or the servicars, but no matter. You'll be able to see how the factory corrected the flaws in this rocker cover or that gearbox.

For more general info, I'm pleased to say the major monthlies are now paying more attention to Harley-Davidson than they used to.

If you really like reading about motorcycles, I heartily recommend *American Racer*, by Steve Wright, and *American Racing Motorcycles*, by Jerry Hatfield. *Harley-Davidson, the Milwaukee Marvel*, by Harry Sucher, is to me overly critical and personal, while David Wright's factory-endorsed *Harley-Davidson Motor Company* is short on technical details and long on praising the factory, but at least the name is spelled right.

As a Harley-Davidson owner you're entitled to receive *The Enthusiast*, the official H-D magazine. As you'd guess, it's firmly on the factory's side but again, it does have reports on new models and accessories, technical tips and a calendar of coming events.

Clubs

First place for clubs must go to the Harley Owner's Group, by no accident shortened to HOG. It's backed and organized by the factory, although you gotta pay dues.

Nicely restored 1953 Hummer is being ridden here by a girl whose right hand is full of ping-pong balls, which she's trying to drop into a row of coffee cans. David Gooley photo.

HOG has all sorts of events like parties before the races so you can meet the team, social events tied into Cycle Week in Daytona Beach, factory tours and patches and deals like renting a Harley for your vacation in Hawaii.

Harley Owners Group
3700 W. Juneau Ave.
Milwaukee, WI 53201

Owning a Harley needn't limit you to the make club. We all should belong to the American Motorcyclist Association. It sanctions the races, and does good work for us all with its government relations department, the network of local chapters and lobbying in our interest.

American Motorcyclists Assn.
PO Box 6114
Westerville, OH 43081-6114

Another activist group is ABATE, A Brotherhood Against Totalitarian Enactments, originally formed to oppose helmet laws. It isn't national in that it doesn't have a national headquarters.

ABATE is a genuine grassroots network of motorcycle fans, lobbying and organizing and voting. Members can be rough diamonds. But you don't have to ride a chopper or sport a tattoo to belong and they do good work. On the cutting edge, you might say. If you find a notice of a nearby meeting, it's worth checking on.

Specialized in a different way is the national old bike club. We here don't own real antiques, but those who do put on swap meets and shows and we're usually welcome there.

Antique Motorcycle Club of America
3431 West Tenth St.
Wichita, KS 67203

Vintage racing has become nationwide, from Daytona Beach to Lodi, Calif. There are several regional groups but the two main clubs are,

American Historic Racing Motorcycle Association
P.O. Box 882
Wausau, WI 54402-0882

This is a starting contest; you leap on the lever, as these guys are doing. Then when it fires, you ride a short way, stop, kill the engine, run a foot race, run back, start again and ride across the finish. Good for the heart! David Gooley photo.

And for dirt,
Vintage Dirt Track Racers Association
4729 S. 31st West Avenue
Tulsa, OK 74107

Both run good clean events and care about the riders and the machines and the sport. I belong to both, and can say only good about them, never mind that I am hopelessly slower than the other riders.

I could go on. For instance, the Retreads is an organization for bike nuts aged beyond forty; the Motor Maids, for women; and the AMA-linked Helpin' Hands, for stranded touring riders. But they're not exactly what this book is here for.

More in our vein, the AMA has regions and within these regions are local clubs. Some are family-based off-road clubs, some mostly race, others tour. When you join the AMA you'll also get a chance to join in these activities. Or not, just as you choose.

Things to do

Lots of clubs, eh? Most people enjoy being around others who like the same thing, in our case, motorcycles. Bike nuts and clubs have been organizing things to do since, one supposes, the first two motorcyclists went for a ride.

I've hinted at some of them. The AMA and its chapters put on road tours all during the riding season. You simply show up and get in line. There are other tours which you complete at your leisure, send in proof you went and get a prize or pin.

The best swap meets are generally held in conjunction with shows. The shows have classes for antique, vintage, veteran, special interest, competition and best of various makes. They have other prizes for longest distance ridden, oldest rider, best unrestored motorcycle and so forth.

With the show and swap meet, there are often field meets. These are not serious contests. There may be a hoop toss, with entrants flinging bicycle tires at hoops ten feet away, or a boot race, where everyone takes off one boot and backs off. The boots are jumbled and the contestants dive into the pile to find their boot, or one that fits. Then they run back, start their machines and cross the finish line.

And there are kick-start contests, slow races, balancing tricks—whatever the organizers can come up with. Because these contests are silly, the winners can brag and the losers don't have to sulk. Fun is what field meets are about.

And that sums up the program. As the T-shirt says,

Get On Your Bike
And Do What You Like
Nobody's ever said it better than that.

Appendix

Letters From Home

When Harley-Davidson went into business, models were identified by year. Then came letters for engines and equipment. Then, and as it's still done, models were known by a sort of code, a series of letters with assigned meanings. It can be confusing, so here's a selection/history, to help keep things clear.

E	the basic version of the big twin.
EL	the E with more power.
F	basic, enlarged from 61 to 74, big twin.
FL	the F with more power.
FLH	still more power and built as Pan, Shovel and Evo.
K	sidevalve middleweight, circa 1952.
KK	tuned version of the K.
KH	the K stroked from 45 to 54 ci.
KHK	tuned version of the KH.
XL	basic Sportster, 1957.
XLC	stripped California model, 1958.
XLH	higher performance XL, 1958.
XLCH	stripped-but-streetable, high-performance XL.
FX	original Super Glide, made from F and X parts.
FXE	same, but with electric start.

That prepares us for the modern era, in which the lines get smudged some.

In the Sportsters, we have:

XLR	souped and stripped XL.
XR-750	iron and alloy 750s, racing only.
XLCR	road race style XLH.
XR-1000	alloy XR top end and dual carbs on the XLH cases.
XLT	an XLH with larger tank.
XLX	stripper/bargain XLH.
XLS	fancier version of the XLH.
XLH	all current Sportsters, 883 and 1200.

The FL line was expanded with the isolation mounts and new frame, fairing and suspension:

FLT	the big touring machine.
FLHT	same, but with the old style fairing.
FLTC	FLT with extras, C standing for Classic.
FLHTC	same as above two, mixed.
FLHS	FLT with windshield and less equipment; S is for Sport.
FLST	Softail with 16-in. front wheel.
FLSTC	same, with windshield.
FLSTF	Fatboy, as in F.
FLSTN	Fatboy with different paint, N meaning Nostalgia.

The Super Glides are the most numerous. The line was used for styling and engineering variations, so there've been . . .

FXS	the original Low Rider.
FXEF	the first Fat Bob, F here for Fat.
FXWG	Wide Glide, with spaced forks and 21 in. front wheel.
FXB	original Sturgis, with B for belt final drive.

FXR	Super Glide II, the original isolation mounting system.
FXRS	an FXR with cast wheels and extra trim, aka Low Glide.
FXSB	Low Rider, with belt drive.
FXST	original Softail.
FXRDG	FXRS with solid disc rear wheel.
FXSTC	Softail Custom.
FXRT	R for rubber mount, T for touring gear but named Sport Glide.
FXRC	Low Glide Custom, plus wire wheels.
FXRT/P	Police equipment on the FXRT.
FXRD	the T equipment plus top box, aka Grand Touring.
FXRS-Sp	the Sports edition of the Low Rider.
FXLR	Low Rider Custom, with 21 in. front wheel.
FXRS-CONV.	Low Rider with detachable windshield and bags.
FXDB	Dyna Glide new system engine mounting, B for belt.
FXDC	same but C for Custom despite no 21 in. front wheel.

Index